US AIR FORCE

IN WORLD WAR II

LOU II
C

US AIR FORCE

IN WORLD WAR II

THOMAS A. SIEFRING

CHARTWELL BOOKS INC.

A BISON BOOK

Published by Chartwell Books Inc., A
Division of Book Sales Inc., 110 Enterprise
Avenue, Secaucus, New Jersey 07094

Second impression 1979

Printed in Hong Kong

ISBN 0-89009-182-X

Library of Congress Catalog
Card Number: 77-88489

CONTENTS

INTRODUCTION by S. L. Mayer

The concept of a history of the United States Air Force in World War II is something of a misnomer. First of all, the USAF was not officially established until 1947, two years after the war came to an end. Until that time the air power of the United States was split between the Army and Navy, although the USAAC (United States Army Air Corps, later called the USAAF (United States Army Air Force), the postwar rump of which became the nucleus of the USAF, was, if not the senior air arm, arguably the more important of the two. In fact, both the US Navy and US Marines played essential roles, particularly in the Pacific, protecting aircraft carriers, attacking the Japanese from those carriers, as well as carrying out vital naval reconnaissance. The strategic bombing offensive, both against Germany and Japan, was carried out largely if not exclusively by the USAAF.

Tom Siefring, the author of the history of the USAAF in World War II, is ideally placed to have written this book. For seven years he has been stationed in the United Kingdom, which, certainly for the European Theater of Operations in World War II, was the crucial command post of the Eighth Air Force. Great Britain now is the center of NATO operations outside Germany and the Third Air Force, stationed for almost twenty years at South Ruislip in Middlesex only a few miles from London, has been moved to its present headquarters at RAF Mildenhall, Suffolk, in East Anglia, from which many operations against Germany and the Nazi-controlled Continent of Europe were directed. The long tradition of American air power in Britain from 1942 to the present day links the histories of the Eighth and the Third. They are part of one story – defense of Britain against a totalitarian enemy on the Continent. Part of this story is told by Sergeant Siefring, who still serves as a non-commissioned officer in the USAF at High Wycombe where he became one of America's most highly decorated men in uniform. In his capacity as air policeman, he won every award that an NCO in his position could have earned, topped by his receipt of the nomination, Policeman of the Year, given in 1976 for his services to both the British government and American military authorities in the United Kingdom.

These awards are most relevant in the context of this book, because the continuing co-operation between the American military establishment in Britain and the British government is indicative of the trust between the two great Anglo-Saxon nations which was forged in the heat of conflict. This mutual trust continues to thrive. When the United States entered World War I American air power was virtually non-existent despite the invention of the Wright Brothers and other early American pioneers of the exploration of heavier-than-air craft. American pilots latterly played a significant role in World War I, but it is significant to note that not one single American-built flying machine ever fought in the skies over France during the Great War. American pilots flew French or British planes. Although American-built aircraft were ready for action in 1919, the war, by that time, was over, and interest in military aircraft diminished in the 1920s. But a tradition of co-operation in wartime between Britain and America was forged. The role of American air forces in World War II was built on this tradition.

Another tradition was created as well. It was an abiding interest in planes and pilots which transcended the period of 'Normalcy' in the US in the 1920s largely characterized by a disinterest of the American people in foreign affairs. Pilots like Charles A. Lindbergh captured the headlines and thrilled two continents. Wiley Post and Amelia Earhart Putnam delighted Americans by their daring achievements in the air and later, saddened them by their tragic, untimely deaths in their attempt to achieve mastery of the air. However pioneers of military air power, like

Billy Mitchell, initially were ignored and even castigated for their beliefs. But increasing growth in domestic air transport, which included transcontinental, 11-stop flights of passengers willing to pay the high cost and endure the inconvenience of flights from New York to Los Angeles, kept the American public aware of the possibilities of mass air transport. When the storm clouds gathered over Europe and Asia in the 1930s, President Franklin Delano Roosevelt quietly began to encourage development of modern war planes which would inevitably be required in another world conflict.

Once more Anglo-American co-operation was the foundation on which the new age of American air power would be built. Aircraft engines for use in British planes were developed both in Canada, under American direction, and in the United States itself. When Britain went to war in 1939, even before the Lend-Lease Act of March 1941, the British and American governments worked closely together to provide for the day when American political isolation would end in the development of aircraft engines, fighters and bombers. When that day came on 7 December 1941, it was only a matter of weeks before American pilots and maintenance personnel were working openly with the Royal Air Force to transfer RAF bases to American control and eventually to airlift tens of thousands of planes and men to join the Mighty Eighth in the UK.

The co-operation between the RAF and the Eighth Air Force occupies a central place in this book. Fighter as well as bomber operations for the USAAF began in Britain, eventually expanding to North Africa, Sicily, Italy and finally France when the final assault against the Third Reich was launched. In the Pacific British and American crews worked side by side in Burma, China and, thanks to Australia's RAAF, throughout the whole of the Pacific Theater as well as the CBI. The immense technical achievements of aircraft designers, pilots and ground crews are still dwarfed by the personal valor of the men that took to the skies and risked their lives daily to achieve victory. No one who has ever experienced the gnawing fear of being attacked by a hail of anti-aircraft fire over Germany or a squadron of Me-109s can fully understand the feelings of a bombardier, co-pilot or tail gunner in a burning B-17. America and Britain paid the price for complacency which lingered well into the 1930s, and the price was numbered in human lives, indomitable courage and omnipresent fear. Vigilance has been a lesson learned the hard way, and the continuing presence of the USAF in Britain and Europe bears witness to it.

As the editor of this book I have a special interest to declare. The US Third Air Force, which took over responsibility for the defense of Britain in 1949, is very close to my heart. I have taught history and international relations at American air bases in Britain for well over a decade for the University of Maryland, the University of Southern California's Graduate School, and the University of Nebraska. Most of my students were, and are, Air Force pilots, ground crews, administrative personnel and their dependents. RAF bases which knew the roar of B-17s and B-24s, such as Alconbury, Mildenhall, Lakenheath and Bentwaters, are familiar to me. They are even more familiar to the author of this book who was my student at the University of Maryland and USC's Graduate School. Both of us would like to dedicate this book to the continuing tradition of Anglo-American co-operation in the skies and on the ground, but more than that, we would like to dedicate the History of the United States Army Air Force in World War II to the men and women of the Eighth and the Third Air Forces, those who have served and those who continue to serve the cause of liberty in Britain and throughout the world. It is they who have helped make us, who have been our friends and colleagues in peace and war, and it is they who help to make the world safe from tyranny and intolerance. Long may they continue to do so.

B-17 Flying Fortresses over Mainz.

Early Years

Below: *American Bill Thaw in the French uniform of the Lafayette Escadrille with flag presented by the US Treasury Department at Soissons in May 1917.*

At its peak strength in World War II, the United States Army Air Force had in excess of 2,370,000 men and women in uniform: pilots, navigators, bombardiers, radio operators, gunners, mechanics, engineers, military policemen, clerks, instructors, statisticians, cooks and many others – it took many specialities to conduct and support the war in the air. All of these men and women, from the lowest to the highest, were welded together into an efficient and effective organization which coordinated and directed the many diverse functions of the Army Air Force. To appreciate fully what the Army Air Force was up against, a brief history of the background and progress of the Air Corps prior to 7 December 1941 is necessary.

On 1 August 1907, the United States Army established the Aeronautical Division of the Signal Corps and acquired its first operational aircraft of French manufacture two years later. At first the Army looked on the new division as someone's fantasy come to life, but nevertheless, went ahead with a training program for pilots. These new aviators were not organized into air units for operational missions. Therefore, when relations with Mexico became strained and reached the breaking point in 1913 as a result of the revolution and overthrow of Juarez, not one US air unit was ready for active service along the troubled Mexican border. However, the Army dispatched several aircraft to Texas which were formed into the 1st Aero Squadron (Provisional), on 5 March 1913. It is interesting that although the United States was the home of the Wright Brothers and the primary promoter of the airplane, not one American manufactured aircraft was in the inventory. At this time, the great US air industry had not yet been born, so the US had to rely on foreign aircraft and equipment. It wasn't long before the US snapped out of this euphoria.

Despite many difficulties, the Aeronautical Division expanded in material, organization and strength. By December 1914 Brigadier General George P Scrivens, Chief Signal Officer, requested that the division be composed of four air squadrons plus a 50 percent reserve and manned by 20 officers and 90 enlisted men. Also, in December 1914 the 1st Aero Squadron moved to San Diego, California for training and was at that time officially designated as an Army Air Squadron. It consisted of 16 officers, 75 enlisted men and eight aircraft, commanded by Captain Benjamin F Foulois, who was later to reach the highest post in the future Air Corps. This small force represented the entire tactical strength of the United States Army. Following Pancho Villa's raid on Columbus, New Mexico in March 1916, Captain Foulois was dispatched

Above: *RE.18 biplane looping at 2000 meters over France.*
Below: *The Morane Parasol.*

Top: *Pilots of the Lafayette Escadrille and French pilots in front of a Nieuport.*
Above: *Pilots of the Lafayette Escadrille admire their two pet lions, 'Whiskey' and 'Soda'. 'Soda' was smaller and female.*

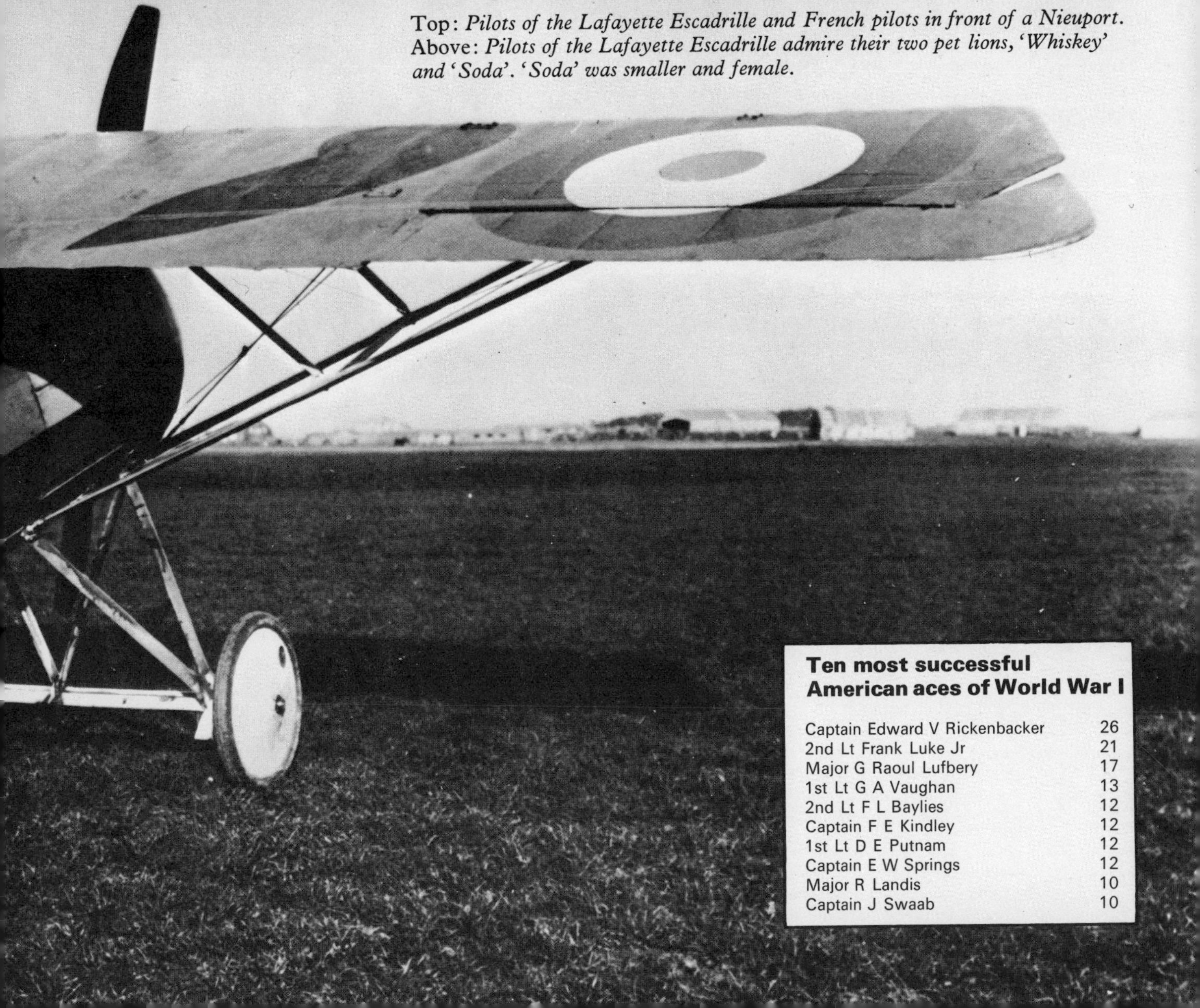

Ten most successful American aces of World War I

Captain Edward V Rickenbacker	26
2nd Lt Frank Luke Jr	21
Major G Raoul Lufbery	17
1st Lt G A Vaughan	13
2nd Lt F L Baylies	12
Captain F E Kindley	12
1st Lt D E Putnam	12
Captain E W Springs	12
Major R Landis	10
Captain J Swaab	10

to Columbus to join Brigadier General John J (Black Jack) Pershing's expeditionary force.

From the beginning they had no real chance of success. Their frail aircraft could not withstand the severe winds, numerous forced landings, dust and snow storms. However, the 1st Aero Squadron was the first US air unit to take part in a military campaign earning a claim to fame. While this escapade was going on, war had broken out in Europe with the assassination of Archduke Franz Ferdinand of Austria but still no progress had been made in preparing the United States for the possibility of her entry into war. Although Congress created the Aviation Section of the Signal Corps on 18 July 1914, the legislators provided little monetary funds for this new service. What money there was became channeled into communications, observations and reconnaissance, instead of the most important aspect – combat. One section of the 2nd Aero Squadron was organized on 1 December 1915 and dispatched to the Philippines. In 1916 plans were already on the table for five additional squadrons. The 3rd, 4th and 5th Aero Squadrons were being formed as the United States entered the war. The 7th Aero Squadron was formed in February 1917 and assigned duty in the Panama Canal Zone. The 6th Aero Squadron was organized in Hawaii in March 1917. It was with this virgin air force that the United States prepared to enter a war which had already cost several million lives and devastated a continent.

In April 1916, the French Air Service established a new *escadrille* (flying squadron), N124 which was destined for great things. It was named *Escadrille Américaine* and was composed entirely of American volunteers, except for its French officers and mechanics. When the war began there were a number of Americans in France, most of whom joined the famous French Foreign Legion. One man who did not, wanted to establish an all-American air squadron; this was Norman Prince of Massachusetts. At first the French government rejected the offer, but after a year of bloody fighting it felt the Americans needed something positive to relate to in this European war. The unit was formed more as a propaganda tool than for its intrinsic military value. One sincerely doubts if it accelerated the US's entry into the war but it was of exceptional propaganda value within the US.

Below: *First Army Wright Type 'C' plane at Fort McKinley in the Philippines in 1912.*

No.

AMERICAN
EXPEDITIONARY FORCES
Corps Expéditionnaire Américain

OFFICER'S IDENTITY CARD
Carte d'Identité d'Officier

Name / Nom: Harlan R. Sumner

Rank / Grade: 1st Lieut. Air Service

Duty / Fonction: Flying

T. B. Bartlett
Capt. C.A.C.

Adjutant General

Signature of Holder

Signature du Titulaire: Harlan R Sumner

Left: *Typical identification card for World War I pilots.*

Below: *Sgt (later Captain) Soubiran at the Cachy Aerodrome, July 1916.*

The Germans immediately lodged a strong protest against the neutral US taking part in the war. The name of the new squadron had to be changed and rather quickly as the US had no desire to be committed to a European conflict over such an issue as the name of a French flying squadron. The first name suggested was *Escadrille des Volontaires*, but the one that finally stuck was the *Escadrille Lafayette* after the famous French general who fought side by side with George Washington during the American Revolution.

The Lafayette Escadrille was only one air squadron and could not possibly absorb all the volunteers. There were 38 Americans in the squadron, and 162 in other units before the US declared war. The American volunteers were called the Lafayette Flying Corps, irrespective of their unit. The Escadrille Lafayette was transferred to the US Air Service, on 18 February 1918, as the 103rd Pursuit Squadron. The unit had recorded a total of 38 victories since its original activation but that was not important; what was of extreme importance was the experience these volunteers had to give to the brand new Air Service.

William Thaw, James N Hall, David Peterson and Raoul Lufbery (the latter credited with 17 victories with the Lafayette Escadrille which was just about 50 percent of their total score) were transferred to the 94th Aero Squadron, commanded by Major John W F M Huffer, a man of vast experience with the Service d'Aéronautique. Alan Winslow, Douglas Campbell and Eddie Rickenbacker were all trained by Raoul Lufbery

Below: *Two Nieuports collided head-on in Pau, France in 1916.*
Above right: *Hangars and airfield of the Lafayette Escadrille at Cachy near the Somme.*

Far left: *French-built Breguets of the 96th Bombardment Squadron head for a daylight bombing assault on Germany in 1918.*
Left: *A Distinguished Service Cross is presented to an American pilot.*

whose training made an enormous impact upon the young airmen of the 94th.

The Escadrille Lafayette recorded the first American to be shot down in World War I. This was H Clyde Balsley who was brought down over Verdun, on 18 June 1916. It also recorded the first American death, when Victor Emanuel Chapman was shot down and killed near Verdun on 23 June 1916. The most noted flyer of the Escadrille Lafayette was Raoul Lufbery who had flown reconnaissance and bomber missions through the winter of 1915–16. When he was approached to join the Escadrille Lafayette because of his American citizenship, he requested a transfer to fighters. He actually joined the Lafayette on 24 May 1916 near Verdun. Two months later after 16 aerial combats, he scored his first victory with a diving attack on an Eindecker (German fighter).

On 8 August Lufbery and Jim McConnell, one of the original members of the Lafayette, were flying on patrol northeast of Verdun, between Douaumont and Vaux, when they became separated. About ten minutes later, Lufbery sighted a German two-seater reconnaissance aircraft which he swiftly brought down. Later on, McConnell heard Lufbery say, 'Poor Bastards'; to obtain his four victories Lufbery flew 29 combat missions. Jim

Above: *A German Rumpler is taken during a photographic mission in 1917.*

McConnell was severely injured a few days later when he crashed in a forced landing. Although hospitalized twice, he insisted on returning to flight duties. He was shot down and killed in March 1917. It was conjectured that the reason for his death was that he was unable to turn around because of his back injuries, allowing an enemy pilot to surprise him. Thus, the Lafayette lost one of its finest airmen. Two other members of the Lafayette who transferred to the 94th were James N Hall and David Peterson. Peterson survived the war with five confirmed victories, but died in an accident a few months after the Armistice. Hall was quite a different individual, a fighter pilot who had a college degree. He fought first with the 9th Battalion, Royal Fusiliers in the trenches at Loos and Messines in 1915 and after his discharge returned to France, enlisting in the Service d'Aeronautique. His first victory was the last recorded by the Escadrille Lafayette.

General Pershing, Commander of the American Expeditionary Forces (AEF), coordinated and developed plans for the deployment of 260 air squadrons to France. This plan was later revised, with a cutback in total squadrons to 202. Pershing saw the Air Service's roles as (1) to drive off enemy aircraft, (2) to maintain air superiority over friendly ground forces, and (3) to obtain information about hostile troop movements. Fifty percent of his air arm were to be observation units assigned to three armies and 16 corps. The other 50 percent were to be composed of 60 pursuit, 27 night bombardment and 14 day bombardment squadrons.

The 1st Aero Squadron which departed in August 1917 from New York arrived at Le Havre on 3 September. It was the first US air unit to reach war-torn France. It was not until February 1918 that the first US air unit entered combat with the French Spad S.13 but by November 20 pursuit, 18 observation and seven bombardment squadrons were committed to the front. The French Spad S.13 equipped 16 pursuit squadrons of the AEF by the end of the war. The other aircraft widely utilized by the US squadrons was the Morane-Saulnier A-1, which was used by the Aviation Section as an advanced trainer. The US air arm played an important role in such battles as the Aisne-Marne, St Mihiel and Meuse-Argonne.

The United States developed extremely slowly in the field of military aviation, primarily as a result of the minute funds allocated by Congress. At the outbreak of World War I, the US Army Air Service only had 20 operational aircraft and 30 trained pilots. By the time the US entered the war in 1917, the situation had not improved at all. It was a credit to the Air Service that it managed to achieve what it did from such a bad start. Although Glenn Curtiss designed flying-boats were utilized by the Royal Naval Air Service, no aircraft of original US design took any part in the fighting. Between the world wars though, the US developed some excellent fighters, both for land and aircraft carrier operations, which led to further design developments in World War II. Finally, once reinstated, it was the United States which led the way in shifting over to the monoplane design for combat aircraft.

In April 1917, when the United States entered the World War I, the country which had pioneered the airplane was definitely far behind its European counterparts. No American aircraft was considered combat ready, and it was decided that the US would build aircraft for training purposes and buy proven combat aircraft from France, Italy and Great Britain. France provided over 4881 aircraft for the US and was by far the largest supplier of aircraft. The Aviation Section began a massive expansion program to compensate for this production deficiency but it was far too ambitious. However, this increase eventually brought US combat operational strength to 740 aircraft by the end of the war. These were mostly made up of Nieuports and Spads. Even then compared to the 3300 British, 4500 French and 2400 German aircraft, the years of idleness were plainly visible. From complete unpreparedness, the Aviation Section went on to put an excellent trained, first-rate air force into battle that was just as good as its contemporaries. The final tally was 781 enemy aircraft destroyed for a loss of 289 of its own – quite an outstanding record.

Left: *One of the first aircraft carriers, HMS* Argus *signaled a total change in naval tactical thinking.*
Below: *Pilots of the Lafayette Escadrille at Ham, France in a cold May in 1917.*
Bottom: *Captain Eddie Rickenbacker stands by his Spad. Note the 'Hat in the Ring' emblem on the fuselage. He recorded 26 kills which made him the top American fighter ace.*

The last year of the Great War saw the precedent for using foreign aircraft reversed and US companies were requested to submit designs for a single-seat fighter to replace the French Spad S.7. The company which produced the first American single-seat fighter was the Thomas-Morse Aircraft Corporation. This new aircraft was the MB-3; it resembled the Spad and became the Air Corps standard pursuit aircraft.

It must be mentioned that although the British aircraft industry had a marvelous production record, it owed a tremendous debt to its French counterpart across the Channel. The French had one of the best organized aircraft industries when war broke out. Every engine in the planes dispatched to Belgium and France in August 1914 by the Royal Flying Corps (RFC) and Royal Naval Air Service (RNAS) was manufactured in France. Even the great British fighters, the Sopwith Camel, Pup and SE 5 continued to use French engines well into 1918.

France produced 67,982 aircraft during the war; Italy produced close to 20,000; and Germany 47,637. The United States, home of the airplane, was so far behind that the Air Service had to utilize other Allied aircraft to supply its air squadrons. The US did build 15,000 aircraft in 21 months of war, but none were ever used in combat. Considering this was accomplished from scratch, it was something to be proud of and led the way to the giant aircraft corporations of 25 years later.

Although utilizing foreign aircraft like the Nieuport 28, Spad and Sopwith Camel, US pilots played an active role in the war. They protected friendly observation balloons and planes, made strafing attacks on enemy ground forces, but primarily engaged the enemy in counter-air patrols. One of the most famous of these World War I

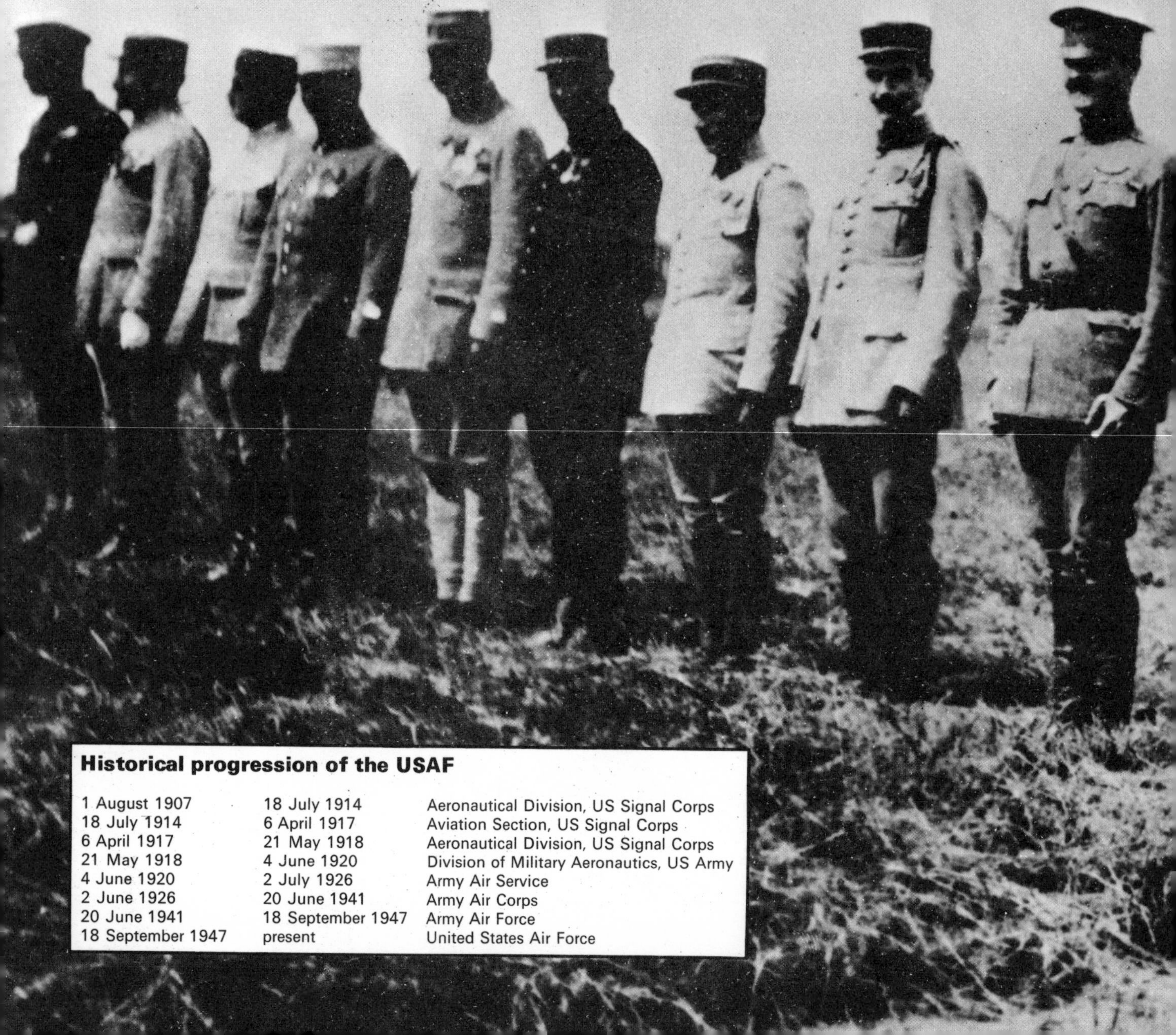

Historical progression of the USAF

1 August 1907	18 July 1914	Aeronautical Division, US Signal Corps
18 July 1914	6 April 1917	Aviation Section, US Signal Corps
6 April 1917	21 May 1918	Aeronautical Division, US Signal Corps
21 May 1918	4 June 1920	Division of Military Aeronautics, US Army
4 June 1920	2 July 1926	Army Air Service
2 June 1926	20 June 1941	Army Air Corps
20 June 1941	18 September 1947	Army Air Force
18 September 1947	present	United States Air Force

pilots was Captain Edward V Rickenbacker, the 'Ace of Aces', who commanded the crack 94th (Hat-in-the-ring) Squadron. On 25 September 1918, near Billy, France, disregarding heavy enemy odds, he attacked a flight of seven aircraft and destroyed two, and was subsequently awarded the Medal of Honor for his courageous act of heroism. Another Medal of Honor winner was 2nd Lt Frank Luke Jr – 'the balloon buster' – who destroyed three German balloons on 29 September 1918 before sustaining damage to his aircraft which forced him to crash land near a small village in northern France, where he died while attempting to resist capture. These are just two of many such airmen who flew combat air missions during World War I. After the surrender of Germany, the US quickly dismantled its military forces. In fact, military services were reduced almost overnight.

Far left: *Philip Parmalee and Lt M S Crissy in a Wright airplane.*
Left: *James McConnell of the Lafayette Escadrille.*
Below: *Officers of 103rd Aero Sqn receive French decorations in 1918. Photos on this page by Capt Soubiran.*

The end of the war brought a need for a workable peace treaty for the vanquished. This was not to be; the Treaty of Versailles was harsh and punitive, the victor dictating to the defeated. No matter how hard President Wilson tried, he could not persuade Lloyd George or Clemenceau to change their minds. His Fourteen Points aimed at a more peaceful settlement than any European statesman was prepared to put forward. The formal signing was in the Hall of Mirrors at Versailles on 28 June 1919; Wilson now had to obtain the Senate's approval. Opposition was already formed before he presented the treaty to the Senate in July 1919. Liberals who had supported the President were disillusioned and critical because the treaty fell far below their idealistic expectations. German-Americans thought it was too hard on Germany. Italian-Americans thought it did not give Italy what had been promised. Irish-Americans thought it was too

Above: *The La Noblette Aerodrome, home of the 103rd Aero Squadron, in February 1919.*
Left: *This Type Morane plane was wrecked, but the pilot escaped injury.*

Personnel strength

1907	3	1927	10,078
1908	13	1928	10,549
1909	27	1929	12,131
1910	11	1930	13,531
1911	23	1931	14,780
1912	51	1932	15,028
1913	114	1933	15,099
1914	122	1934	15,861
1915	208	1935	16,247
1916	311	1936	17,233
1917	1,218	1937	19,147
1918	195,023	1938	21,089
1919	25,603	1939	23,455
1920	9,050	1940	51,165
1921	11,649	1941	152,125
1922	9,642	1942	764,415
1923	9,441	1943	2,197,114
1924	10,547	1944	2,372,292
1925	9,670	1945	2,282,259
1926	9,674		

favorable to Great Britain. Widespread isolationism and nationalism assured objections to the League Covenant. This was the political state in which the Air Service attempted to flex its newly found wings and obtain additional funds for personnel, equipment, training, research and development.

President Wilson was one of the most learned men ever to hold the office of President. His doctorate in history, however, was focused on domestic matters and not on foreign affairs and this fact hindered him in his dealings with the great European nations. He led the US successfully before and during the war but he could not obtain the Senate's approval for the ratification of the Treaty of Versailles or to join the League of Nations. With a Republican majority in Congress, the US was well on its way to isolationism.

After Wilson, Warren G Harding was President from 1921 until his death in August 1923. He campaigned for 'normalcy' and most Americans wanted just that, a return to the normal *status quo*. The people and politicians did not realize that isolationism was a thing of the past: to divorce oneself from the rest of the world was impossible. In 1921 the US made a separate peace with Germany in an agreement similar to the Versailles Treaty but without the League of Nations Covenant. Thus ended all of Wilson's hopes and expectations for an association of states. This period from 1921–29 was a period of semi-dor-

Above: A Bleriot with two 110hp and two 120hp Rhone motors.
Left: *Parisians acclaim the arrival of General John J Pershing, June 1917. He appears in the inset.*

mancy for the Air Service. Individual airmen and their deeds set the pace but the Air Service as an entity virtually stood still. Funds were just not available for any of the programs which were vitally needed.

Thus isolationism became the US policy of the day. Americans did not enjoy fighting European wars. If the Europeans were big enough to start a war, they should be big enough to finish it. This was the sentiment of most Americans who turned their backs on Europe during the 1920s. In so doing they inadvertently turned their backs on aircraft development and the nascent air power of the USA.

Below: *General Billy Mitchell and a French officer in a Spad.*

Dawn to dusk flight by Lt Russell L Maughan in a Curtiss PW-8 in February 1923. This flight was unsuccessful but a second attempt on 23 June 1924 worked well.

The Locust Years

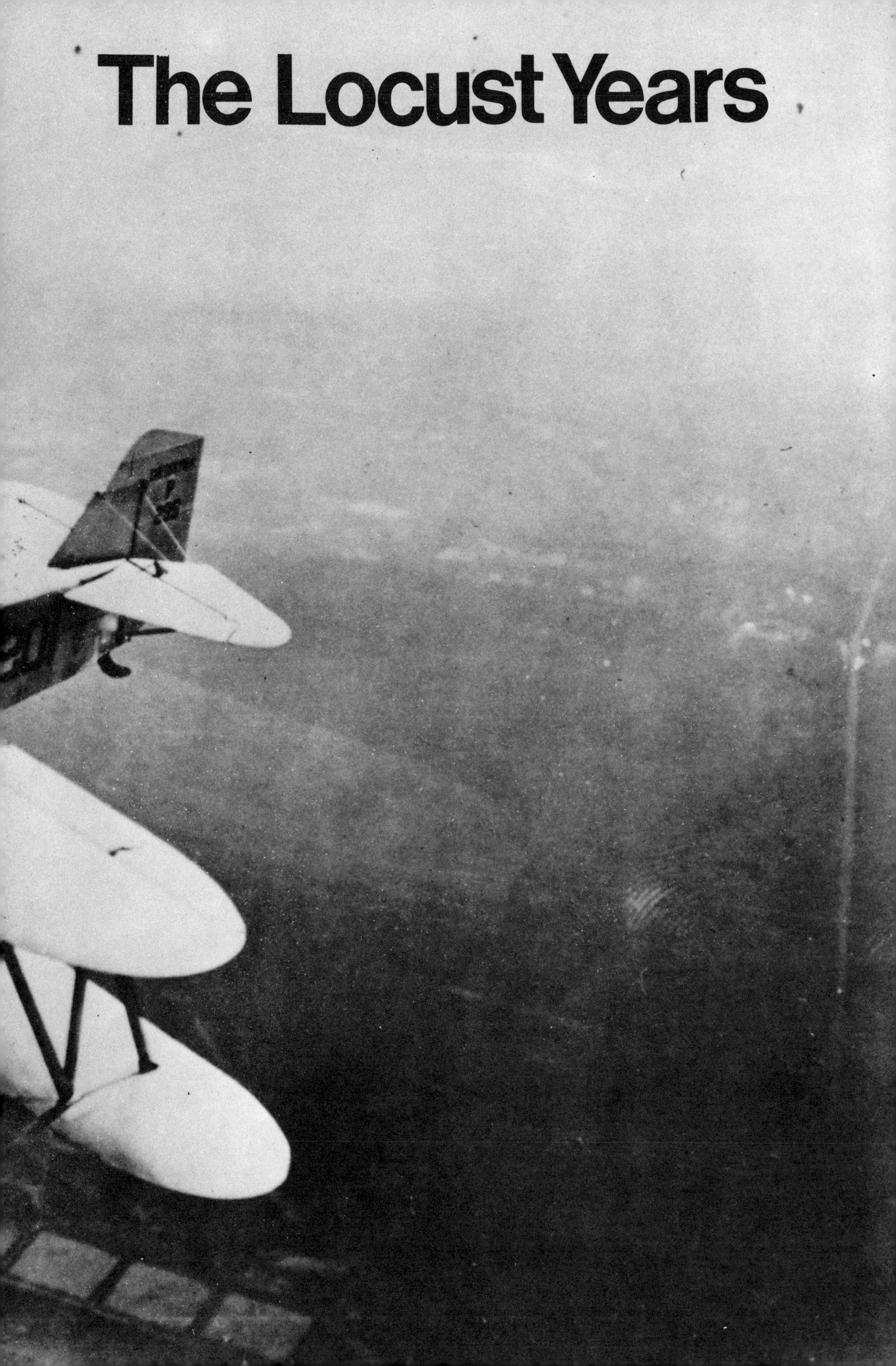

With the end of the war, the now veteran Air Service was demobilized, from 200,000 men to less than 10,000 by 30 June 1920. The aircraft industry which had for a brief span become a corporate giant dwindled to a fraction of its former self. From 1920–30 there was practically no progress and the Air Service was forced to utilize leftover parts and spares for their few remaining aircraft.

An important postwar task was the reorganization of the Air Service itself. The Army Reorganization Act of 1920 made the Air Service an integral part of the US Army with an authorized strength of 1511 officers and 16,000 airmen. The Air Service was given control of research and development (R&D) with the authority to buy its own aircraft and other related equipment. A more difficult problem to resolve was the potential of air power in any future war. The leading proponent of the new theory of strategic bombing and a strong air service was Brigadier General William Mitchell. He was an outstanding airman, outspoken champion of strategic bombing and airpower. He gained much valuable experience in France during the war. Mitchell believed the defense of the US should not rest with the US Navy but with the Air Service, which inevitably resulted in bad feelings between both services.

Mitchell carried out tests in July 1921, utilizing Martin NBS-1 aircraft of the Air Service which resulted in the sinking of three ex-German capital ships of the line anchored in Chesapeake Bay. The most notable of the trio was the *Ostfriesland*, the allegedly unsinkable battleship. This was repeated in September 1923 when two US battleships were sunk off Cape Hatteras, North Carolina. But as usual, instead of winning support, Mitchell only succeeded in antagonizing the military hierachy, and was dispatched to the Philippines for an inspection tour to cool off. He did just the opposite making matters worse. He made General Summerall, the commander of the Hawaiian Department 'fit to be tied', by publicly denouncing his apparent inattention to the air defenses of Oahu. This did not endear him to his opponents as Summerall was in line for the coveted Army Chief of Staff position.

Of course Mitchell's followers were ecstatic at the results of his bombing trials and the evidence he was uncovering in his recent inspections; it looked as if finally evidence was building up in favor of the Air Service's claim to be the leader of future strategy and tactics. However, US Naval prestige and power, plus Congressional backing, outweighed the arguments and hypotheses of the Mitchellites. The revolutionary concept of air power for national defense was nipped in the bud. A point was taken from these tests in favor of the Navy; the aircraft carrier eventually became the principle weapon at sea.

Mitchell, meanwhile undaunted by the turn of events, continued his campaign for air power. His criticism of the Air Service was completely valid: for example, there were 2796 aircraft in service or temporary storage, the majority of which were obsolete. Mitchell could not see how the Air Service could stand the rate of peacetime casualties which had occurred. From 1 June through 30 June 1921, 69 officers died and 27 were severely injured in over 330 air crashes.

By July 1924 the Air Service had 754 aircraft of which 457 were observation, 78 pursuit, 50 bombers, eight attack and 152 trainers. Chief of Air Service, Major General Mason M Patrick, put forward a tentative recommendation for 80 percent combat and 20 percent observation aircraft. As usual funds were not available to bring about the necessary changes, and General Patrick believed that what little funds were available should be channeled into research and development projects to find the best possible aircraft for the future. Then, if and when the US became involved in another war, the best design could be mass-produced.

Left: *A moonlight reconnaissance flight over the sea.*
Right: *A formation of Boeing P-12s flown by members of the 27th Pursuit Squadron of Selfridge Field near Mount Clemens, Michigan.*

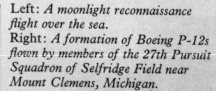

Above: *A Douglas B-7 light bomber is checked by ground crews.*

In April 1925, the Mitchell saga came to a stirring conclusion; Mitchell was transferred from his position as Assistant Air Chief to Corps Air Officer at San Antonio, Texas. On 5 September, he made comments to the press that the loss of a US Naval airship was due to inexcusable negligence by naval aviation leaders, and simultaneously attacked the Army's high command for its lack of foresight in regard to the potential of the Air Service. These outspoken comments and his hot temper resulted in a general court-martial on eight charges of violating the Articles of War. The inevitable result was reached and he was suspended from the Air Service, and retired soon afterwards.

Above: *General Mitchell and his staff at Koblenz, 15 January 1919.*

The Air Service continued with its experimentations for the best possible all-round aircraft, the most successful were the Barling bomber, a six-engined triplane, weighing in excess of 42,000lbs; and the Curtiss Condor NBS-4, twin-engined bomber, which had a speed slightly faster than 100 mph. However, the Air Service placed emphasis on the development and production of pursuit aircraft. The most important of these were the Curtiss PW-8 Hawk, a single-engine aircraft capable of 178mph at 22,000ft and the Curtiss A-3 Falcon which was used for low-level ground support.

The Air Service strived for independence through the 1920s but although supported by the Lassiter Board and the Lampert Committee of the House of Representatives, this was not to be. In September 1925, President Calvin Coolidge appointed Dwight Morrow to chair another board. The Morrow Board unlike its predecessors was firmly against an independent air arm but did recommend that the Air Service be redesignated the Air Corps for additional prestige. This was accepted by Congress and the new designation became effective on 2 July 1926. In 1926 the Board's findings justified the authorization for a five year expansion program which was not implemented until July 1927. The immediate objective was a force of 1650 officers, 15,000 airmen and an optimistic 1800 aircraft during the five-year span. The Air Corps did not achieve this planned objective but only because of appropriation cuts averaging 40 percent over the five-year period. By June 1932, it had a force of 1305 officers, 13,400 airmen and 1709 aircraft, a considerable improvement from the days gone by.

The many achievements of the Air Corps did much to put it in the limelight. On 28 June 1927, Lts Lester J Maitland and Alfred H Hegenberger made the first nonstop flight from Oakland, California to Hawaii in a Fokker C-2 monoplane. Between 1–7 January 1929, Major Carl A Spaatz, Captain Ira C Eaker and Lt Elwood R Quesada established a world endurance record in a three-engined Fokker C-2A, named *Question Mark* utilizing a flight refueling technique pioneered by the Air Service in 1923. In September 1929 Lt James Doolittle made the first blind solo flight at Mitchell Field, New York. He flew a 15 mile circuit and landed in zero visibility without a single mishap. The early 1930s saw Doolittle break record after record; in fact, he became a regular on the front page of most newspapers across the country.

On 12 April 1930 Captain H M Elmendorf, commander of the 95th Pursuit Squadron, set an altitude record of 30,000ft. The next aerial feat was the first blind solo flight made completely by instruments, accomplished by Captain Hegenberger at Wright Field, Dayton, Ohio. The Air Corps's most important aircraft of this period was the Martin B-10 bomber, a twin-engined, monoplane bomber which was introduced in June 1934. The B-10B featured an enclosed cockpit, a manually rotated gun-turret in the nose, a 2260lb bomb capacity and three 0.30in guns. It was powered by two Pratt and Whitney R1820-33 radial engines with a maximum speed of 213mph at 24,000ft and an overall range of 1240 miles.

On 19 July, a test flight was scheduled and ten of these bombers lifted off from Bolling Field, Washington DC en route to Fairbanks, Alaska, commanded by Lt Colonel Henry H (Hap) Arnold. On 20 August they

Above: *Inspection of the* Frankfurt *after a 4th bombing attack, 18 July 1921.*

touched down at Seattle, Washington, after completing a round trip of 8290 miles and one leg of almost 900 miles nonstop from Juneau to Seattle. The achievements of the Air Corps during this period completed their formative years. They gained experience and irreplaceable confidence flying reliable aircraft which had proved the benefits of a firm and progressive research and development program.

The B-9 and B-10 bombers created new possibilities for the Air Corps. The performance of the B-10 now was better than its contemporary pursuit aircraft. The senior air officers were beginning to realize fully the potential of strategic bombing. A heavy bomber capable of independent action theoretically could more than hold its own against pursuit aircraft. The opponents of strategic bombardment now had to rehash their objections in the face of this new aircraft.

Prior to the 1930s the United States still relied heavily upon foreign manufactured aircraft. But by the 1930s American companies started developing in their own right. The companies which had the primary responsibility for fighter designs through this period were the Boeing and Curtiss Corporations. Curtiss was already involved in fighter production when his company was selected to manufacture the British designed SE 5a. The US Army Engineering Division had their own ideas about designs which resulted in the Orenco D, the first single-seat fighter of completely American design. The Orenco Ds did not see active service because the MB-3 was taken instead, but nonetheless it was a positive step forward. Curtiss's next step was to build small biplane fighters contracted by the Naval Aircraft Factory, for use aboard the *USS Langley*, the first US aircraft carrier. A fighter of Curtiss's own design finally appeared in 1924. This was the PW-8, first of the famous Hawk line. Lt Russell Maugham flew one of these original Hawks from Mineola, Long Island to San Francisco, on the 24 June 1924, in only 21 hours, 48 minutes. One of the first production aircraft in 1925 was modified to have a turned-type radiator fitted under the nose and was designated the P-1 Hawk. The US Navy also ordered the new P-1, but wanted an air-cooled radial engine which was designated F-6C. The Curtiss Hawk fitted either with a Curtiss, Wright or Pratt and Whitney engine was widely used until 1935. The P-6 was the last in the series. Instead of water in the cooling system, ethylene glycol was used which enabled the radiator for the V-1570 Curtiss engine to be made much smaller. The P-6E was the last biplane fighter bought by the Army Air Corps.

Curtiss continued to develop series of multi-purpose aircraft for aircraft carriers. In 1932 he produced the Goshawk F-11C, a single-seat fighter-bomber. The F-11C was developed from the F-6C and P-6E, and was the last biplane model to serve with the US Navy. The next step for the now amalgamated Curtiss-Wright Corporation was to design a monoplane single-seat fighter when it became apparent that the Hawk series was limited for future

Above: *USS* Alabama *suffers damage from two 25lb white phosphorous bombs delivered by a bomber from Langley Field, Virginia.*
Left: *A 300lb demolition bomb hits the* Alabama *in Chesapeake Bay in 1921.*

expansion. The P-36 was the result. This design model was called the P-36A Mohawk IV. It had a 1050hp Pratt and Whitney engine, weighed 4541lbs, with a maximum speed of 303mph and a range of 680 miles. The Mohawk was submitted for contract in May 1935 and put into production in 1938. The largest buyer was the French *Armée de l'Air* which outfitted five groups by May 1940.

During the same period of industrial expansion, the Boeing Company was also producing some of the finest military aircraft of the decade. Its single-seat fighter, the FB-1, was a biplane with a steel-tube, fabric-covered fuselage and wooden wings. The Army Air Corps ordered a moderate number of this model which was used throughout the period between the wars. Radial engines were added to the US Navy production model in 1926 which led to the development of a new fighter for carrier operations. These were the F2B and F3B fighter-bombers, powered by a Pratt and Whitney R-1340B radial engine, armed with two forward firing machine guns and carrying up to 125lbs of bombs. But Boeing's greatest achievement between 1928 and 1933, was the F4B; 586 were constructed which set a production record for a single American aircraft. It was designed to meet the specifications and requirements of both services. Although a major supplier of fighters between the wars, Boeing gained its fame for its bomber line. In 1931, the B-9 bomber went into production and became the outstanding bomber of that time with a semi-retractable undercarriage and variable pitch propellers which gave it the same speed and climb as the most contemporary fighters. The first fighter to be modified with these features was the P-26 which was ordered by the Air Corps in 1933.

The success of the P-26 resulted in a design competition for a new all-metal monoplane fighter with an enclosed cockpit and retractable undercarriage. The contract was won by the Seversky Company for its P-35, designed by Alexander Kartuli. The last in the series was the P-47 Thunderbolt, one of the most famous fighters of World War II. The P-35 was originally built as a two-seater, but because of the required speed of 250mph it was rebuilt as a single-seater. It was powered by a twin Wasp engine that assured a maximum speed of 250mph at 10,000ft.

During the period between the wars politics was very much involved in the progression, expansion and modernization of the Air Corps. Four months before the stock market crash in October 1929, President Hoover ordered General Summerall to conduct a survey of possible economy cuts which could be taken without gravely damaging national defense. That, of course, was an impossible situation as it was already grossly inadequate. Summerall solicited reports from his area and department commanders for recommendations on reductions in spending. General Douglas MacArthur sent a reply to the effect that he could not see any way to cut his already diminished expenses in his department. He did recommend that the US garrison in China be redeployed due to the existing turmoil between Russian and Chinese forces along the Manchurian border. The General Staff's report in December 1929, in regard to the Philippines, stated that the mission was to hold the Manila area until the arrival of reinforcements and was to organize a native Filipino Army to augment the US garrison in the event of a wartime contingency. This plan to raise such a force was precluded by the world-wide depression which shook the earth's economic core.

Between 1920–30 the US had become the leading industrialized nation in the world and had only its own wave of economic nationalism to blame for the Great Depression. There were warnings that a change was occurring in the economy. The residential construction industry slumped in 1928. This was the beginning and Hoover attempted to stem the tide by reversing the relatively easy monetary policies of Coolidge and Mellon. But the die was cast; on 24 October 1929, 'Black Thursday', the stock market collapsed. This was the political, economic and social millstream with which the Air Corps had to contend until the late 1930s. Always operating with a deficit it was felt that someone had to take a cut in funds, and the opinion of the older services was that it should be the Air Corps.

In 1930 the Great Depression was starting its second year. If President Hoover is remembered for anything it is for bank failures, high unemployment, falling industrial production and the lowest earnings of the populace for

quite some time. The American economy was infected and it needed a strong shot of antibiotics to snap out of its decline. In early 1931, at this critical point, Lt General Douglas MacArthur took over as Chief of Staff. It seemed then, as today, that Congress was constantly cutting appropriations to the military. The federal budget for the fiscal year 1932 was submitted to Congress before Christmas 1930. The War Department requested $351 million for the military, an $11 million cut, most of which came from the Air Corps. The Federal Budget Bureau, however, incensed the outgoing Chief of Staff, General Summerall, and the entire General Staff by increasing the Air Corps portion at the expense of the ground echelon and civilian compo-

Top: *Dirigibles inspect the* Ostfriesland *at 1115 hrs, 21 July 1921.*
Above: *The* Ostfriesland *going down at 1239 hrs.*
Below: Ostfriesland *sinks without trace a few minutes later.*

nents which were cut back by a further $8 million. This was only the beginning of more subsequent cuts in military appropriations as the depression worsened.

MacArthur developed a close relationship with President Hoover and Secretary of War Hurley. These three men believed in the rugged individualism of the US which set it apart from a degenerate Europe. Europe could only fall back on socialism; the US was to Hoover composed of idealistic individuals who were dynamic in all regards, and who would triumph through social responsibility and equal opportunity. Therefore, Hoover was skeptical of proposals for federal relief and intervention in the economy because this might constitute a threat to individualism and liberty.

In 1931 General MacArthur and Admiral William V Pratt, the Chief of Naval Operations, attempted to end a ten-year dispute dealing with air defense of the coasts. The agreement stated that 'the naval air force will be based on the fleet. . . . The army forces will be land-based and employed as an essential element to the army in the performance of its mission to defend the coasts both at home and overseas.'

The War Department asked for $331 million for the military budget of 1933 but the figure was cut by $15 million again. The new Chief of the Air Corps, Major General Benjamin F Foulois argued vehemently for more funds for military aviation. Also Foulois and Mr Trubee Davison, Assistant Secretary of War for Air, raised the question of the need for separate departmental status for the Air Corps. Franklin D Roosevelt, Governor of New York, pressured by powerful National Guard interests, wrote to New York congressional delegates about the proposed cuts to the National Guard. All was ineffectual and a further cut of $24 million was taken from the military budget that year. It was this interservice rivalry with which the Air Corps had to contend through the 1930s.

By 1932, both General MacArthur and Admiral Pratt were at loggerheads over the types of aircraft each service should have available. The importance of the MacArthur–Pratt Agreement was that the Army became responsible for coastal defense as long as the pact lasted. Thus MacArthur was responsible for the assignment of coastal defense to the Air Corps, and the air arm believed this was a good opportunity to develop a long-range bomber to accomplish this task. In 1935 the Boeing Company came out with the first prototype of the B-17 and by 1936 the Army bought 13 B-17s. Without MacArthur's approval in 1933 for the programmed development of a long-range bomber, the Air Corps would have been at a distinct disadvantage at the outbreak of World War II.

Roosevelt's election in 1932 was to usher in a new day for the armed forces. He definitely favored the Air Corps and Navy, shown by the passage of the

Above: *Formation of Douglas B-18As.*

Merchant Marine Act of 1936, which strengthened the Navy considerably. General MacArthur was retained as Chief of Staff by Roosevelt because of political as well as military reasons. Although MacArthur had enemies, he had more friends on Capitol Hill than many people realized. Roosevelt gave him another chance to fight with Congress over the needs of the Army; he fought hard to save the Army from becoming the economic sacrificial lamb. The military still took a $51 million cut but it was a sight better than the proposed $80 million.

MacArthur was to retire in 1935 as Chief of Staff and was offered a new post as military advisor to the newly formed Philippine Commonwealth, headed by Manuel Quezon, his very close friend. He was not supposed to be formally relieved until 15 December 1935 but while Secretary of War George H Derns was in Manila, Roosevelt announced the appointment of General Malin Craig as the new Chief of Staff on 2 October 1935. This did not actually improve the relationship between MacArthur and Roosevelt but nevertheless MacArthur sent his congratulations to Craig. He had more important things to worry about, getting the Philippines' Armed Forces

Right: *A Westland Limousine equipped with one 250hp Rolls-Royce engine.*
Below: *Lt J A Macready in this LePère aircraft made a record altitude flight from McCook Field in 1921.*
Below right: *The Verville Packard which flew in the Gordon Bennett race.*

Left: *War Minister General Pertine greets US pilots who had just completed their flight to Buenos Aires, Argentina in Boeing B-17s. US Ambassador Alexander Weddell stands at the left.*
Below: *Formation of Curtiss P-6Es flown by pilots of 17th Pursuit Squadron, Selfridge Field, Michigan.*

molded into a challenging fighting force.

One thing that came out of MacArthur's planning was the 1936 military budget which was $361 million, the largest in five years. The military leaders were hoping that Roosevelt was aware of expanding international tensions. The Air Corps was to receive $45 million, an increase of 65 percent over the previous year, and this expansion was to continue until the war.

During 1935 the Air Corps implemented the Baker Board's recommendation that a General Headquarters (GHQ) Air Force be established to control the air arm's combat elements. This was accomplished on 1 March 1935, at Langley Field, Virginia and was commanded by Brigadier General Frank M Andrews who chose his staff carefully from the advocates of air power. His first recommendation was the immediate formation of an East and West Coast bomber group requiring 50 B-17s. This request was refused by the General Staff because the Douglas B-18 was considered to be more than adequate. The real reason though was the lack of funds available for new production. In 1939 when the Luftwaffe launched their massive air attack against Poland, the US Army Air Corps had only 23 B-17 bombers in their entire inventory.

President Roosevelt was determined to keep the US out of any major conflict. Roosevelt's New Deal policy was not alleviating the depression but an expanded military program would provide jobs for people and would aid in the overall economic recovery of the nation. The US was in no position to fight a world war in 1937. The Air Corps was ranked sixth in the world and this was rather disconcerting after it had proved itself so well.

In 1938 it was virtually impossible to convince anyone of the need for long-range bombers which the Air Corps had so painstakingly developed mainly because the US was more isolationist than ever. In 1938 the Secretary of War directed the Air Corps to procure only attack, light and medium bombers in fiscal year 1940. Major General Stanley D Embruck, Deputy Chief of Staff stated the General Staff feeling on heavy bombers:

(a) Defense of the sea areas, other than coastal zones is definitely a function of the Navy.

(b) National policy dictates preparation for defensive action not aggression.

(c) Superiority of a B-17 over other smaller aircraft procured is still to be proven.

To make matters worse, the GHQAF was abolished and Brigadier General Andrews and his key personnel were absorbed into the Air Corps. At this point, President Roosevelt became aware of the strategic possibilities of air power. He advised Congress in January 1939 that 'our existing air forces are so utterly inadequate that they must be immediately strengthen-

Right: *President Calvin Coolidge greets pilots of the Pan-American flight on the day they arrived at Bolling Field, 2 May 1927.*
Below right: *The trimotor Fokker monoplane* Question Mark *being refueled over Burbank, California during its World Endurance Record flight in 1929.*

ed.' Congress reacted by authorizing $300 million to provide 6000 aircraft and to revitalize the Air Corps. This public, Congressional and Presidential confidence in the future potential of air power changed the Army's attitude and objections to the Air Corps. In March 1939 a step had been taken in this direction, when an Air Board made a thorough study of the best means of using air power for national defense. General George C Marshall commented on the board's findings by stating, 'for the first time a specific mission for the Air Corps' has been established. It was ironic that the day of General Marshall's review, 1 September 1939, saw Hitler's Luftwaffe strike through Poland like a sickle at harvest time. It took 32 years continuous fighting before the Air Corps finally achieved a place in our military establishment but even then it had still not achieved complete independence.

The outbreak of hostilities which resulted in the Second World War

Above: *Pan-American flight ships* Detroit, San Francisco *and* St Louis *pass over Duarte Island en route to Colombia.*

shook the US to the core. Complacency and isolationism were now words of the past; the future was very much at stake. The United Kingdom had only $4½ billion in various investments at the start of the war. The only way these funds could be increased was through efforts to export goods such as fine woolens, pottery and whiskey, to the US. Through these exports another $2 million was raised during the next 16 months. But all this was spent when Roosevelt called Congress into a special session to remove the embargo on arms shipments, which although impartial, deprived Great Britain and France of all the advantages of command of the seas in the transportation of supplies. The Neutrality Act was repealed in November 1939 and was replaced by the 'Cash and Carry' principle of which the British took full advantage.

During this period, from Munich to the declaration of war, Great Britain had increased aircraft production enormously. The French, on the other hand, failed to visualize the importance of air power in the coming war. In 1939 Great Britain and France ordered 2500 aircraft of various types from the United States; by the beginning of 1940, the order was increased to 8240 aircraft. These orders plus our own Air Corps requirements boosted air industry production to heights never before reached.

In April 1940, German troops crossed the unguarded Danish border and in a few hours Danish independence was eliminated. Two days later Norway was firmly gripped by a Nazi occupation force. The Allies never recovered from this strike. On 10 May, Hitler's hordes again struck, this time across the Belgian and Dutch frontiers. By 15 May, German Panzers had smashed through the lightly defended Ardennes and dashed across northern France. On the 16th, Roosevelt – alert, calm, confident – practically nonchalantly asked Congress for a billion dollars for defense. He took everyone by surprise when he established a goal of 50,000 planes a year. A politician through and through, Roosevelt had Congress where he wanted it. Swayed by massive public opinion Congress voted these funds and more.

In August 1940 an agreement was concluded between the United States and Great Britain which gave the US permission to build facilities for naval and air bases in Bermuda, the Bahamas, Newfoundland, Jamaica, St Lucia, Trinidad and British Guiana. These bases would be purchased or acquired on a 99 year lease in return for naval vessels, munitions, aircraft and even more important, credit.

Prime Minister Churchill was very interested in the US reinforcing British domestic capacity to manufacture combat aircraft. In fact, Churchill asked Roosevelt for 2000 combat aircraft a month which went up to 3600 a month by July 1942, the preponderance of which would be heavy bombers to destroy the industrial foundations of German military power.

This request rendered the US aircraft industry the largest producer of aircraft in the world.

By September 1940 the US and Britain had started outlining requirements and details for the beginning of aid to the beleaguered British Isles. Six months later Britain received 50 World War I destroyers, five B-17 bombers, over 250,000 rifles and five million rounds of ammunition. This was given in return for long-term leases to build US bases in various British possessions in the Western Hemisphere. On 10 January 1941 the Lend-Lease bill was formally introduced into Congress as House Resolution 1776. It was finally passed on 11 March, assuring continued American material assistance to Britain.

General Henry H Arnold made an offer to the British Air Staff to allocate one-third of the rapidly expanding pilot training courses in the US to British students. Initially 550 were dispatched for training in June and another 550 were sent as soon as the first group graduated. This showed the excellent coordination which was increasing everyday between the USAAF and the RAF. In April 1941

Roosevelt advised Churchill that the US was extending the present security zone, and planned to base aircraft and naval vessels in Greenland, Nova Scotia, Newfoundland, Bermuda and the West Indies. To follow up on the most recent developments in Europe, the War Department established the Special Observer Group in London, and through its reports and those of occasional special missions, the Air Corps was completely informed of the latest material developments in England.

Right: *Formation of Martin B-12s. of the 11th Bombardment Squadron.* Below: *Major Harold L George and members of the seven-man crew of the South American flight from Miami, Florida to Buenos Aires, Argentina stand before their B-17. The flight took eleven days, 16–27 February 1938.*

143
143

The end of May saw the USAAF pilots start flying American built aircraft from factories in the States to Botwood, Newfoundland and turn them over to RAF pilots. This policy changed when Iceland terminated its connection with Denmark on 17 May 1941. Roosevelt then sent US Marines to garrison Iceland on 5 June as a deterrent to a possible Nazi invasion and thus the USAAF pilots flew aircraft to airfields in Iceland where RAF pilots picked them up for transfer.

The US acquired additional bases of operation in Grand Canary, Cape Verde Islands and one of the Azores. The USAAF was beginning to obtain airfields in very strategic locations. The Army conducted a survey to consider the feasibility of ferrying heavy bombers from Natal utilizing three landing fields – Bathurst, Freetown and Liberia – in early June 1941 but Roosevelt did not see the need for long-term leases. With the fall of Denmark, Holland, Norway, Belgium and France, and the Battle of Britain going in full swing, the US became worried about national defense, and rightly so, with the German war machine advancing in all directions. The immediate answer was the Air Force. On 11 September 1941 the Secretary of War and the Secretary of the Navy made a joint report on the forecast of air requirements to wage a war against Japan and Germany. This realistic forecast listed a requirement of 239 combat groups, 63,467 aircraft and 2,164,916 airmen by 1944; the actual number of men used in 1945 was 2,400,000.

The US air industry went from ground zero to the largest in the world. It was producing by far the best fighters and bombers in the world and in bulk. Politics, economics and the Great Depression all had some effect upon the Air Corps, but it survived and went on to play a decisive role in the defeat of Germany and Japan. It was a dream that Billy Mitchell would have enjoyed seeing come true.

Left: *Lt Col 'Hap' Arnold receives the key to Fairbanks in 1934.*
Below: *A DH mail plane in the 1930s.*
Bottom: *B-17s flying to Buenos Aires from Miami for the inauguration of President Roberto Ortiz, 1938.*

Above: *Boeing B-17s of the 8th Air Force in practice formation over England.*

Bombs Away

What exactly is strategic bombing? It is usually defined as a direct attack against an enemy's war-making potential, industries, communications and civilian morale. The object is to totally undermine the enemy's war effort. Strategic bombing was not a new idea born of World War II, but a leftover from the First – the only difference being it was not employed on such a large scale until World War II. Yet for the first half of the war, the bombing was largely ineffective. Serious operational difficulties were encountered from the outset. During the early months, day bomber losses were so severe that the daylight bombing offensive was halted so that by early spring 1940, the offensive was carried out entirely by night. Darkness gave the bombers a cover to evade enemy fighters, but with nothing save the most primitive methods of navigation, the crews experienced great difficulty in locating their targets and returning home. The ultimate result was that the greatest part of the bombing effort was wasted.

Air power was the decisive factor in the defeat of the Axis. The progress made by American manufacturers in aeronautical engineering, developed the aircraft, equipment and weapons that focused attention upon high-altitude precision bombing attacks during the 1930s. The strategic bombing theorists pressing for the development of heavy bombers had to combat the US Navy through the 1930s, which still had implicit faith in its battleship fleet. Even Admiral William D Leahy believed that 'battleships were the best modern weapon.'

In 1931 a significant agreement took place between General Douglas MacArthur, Army Chief of Staff and Admiral Pratt, Chief of Naval Operations, giving the Air Corps responsibility for the land-based defense of the United States and her territories. The Air Corps saw this as an opportunity to exploit the situation and develop a strategic bomber. But this agreement was shortlived; in May 1938 the Chiefs of Staff decided that land-based aircraft should be limited to an off-shore radius of 100 miles; this removed the justification for the long-range heavy bomber. The Air Corps' program for the development of a heavy bomber was immediately canceled.

Therefore, at the start of 1939 the role of the Army Air Corps was clouded and was not yet committed to strategic bombing. About this time President Roosevelt became anxious about Germany's expansion into Austria and the Sudetenland. He was especially alarmed at the Luftwaffe's obvious strength, as he could foresee the possibility of American involvement in Europe. In an address to Congress in January 1939, Roosevelt stated that 'our air forces are so utterly inadequate that they should be immediately strengthened.' This secured a grant of $300 million for the Air Corps to expand to a force of 5500 aircraft by 30 January 1941.

On 1 September 1939 Hitler unleashed his blitzkrieg against Poland; also on that day, the role of the Air Corps changed to include the whole Western Hemisphere. Obviously, a long-range aircraft would be necessary and the advocates of strategic bombing again managed to get their feet in the door.

Despite the numerous uncertainties of changing policy, the research and development work had been forging ahead during the 1930s. This resulted in the Martin B-10, an all-metal, twin-engined monoplane which was very successful. Meanwhile Boeing was pushing with its 29 model, four-engined prototype bomber. The Army Air Corps called it XB-17, and it was to become the most famous bomber of World War II. At practically the same time the B-17B was put into production. Consolidated Air Corporation's B-24 was flying its test flights in December 1939. Although the B-24 had a greater bomb capacity and a longer range than the B-17, it was proven slower at high altitudes and had much less fire power. It was never as effective in the strategic bombing operations in Europe as the B-17.

In the summer of 1940 talks began

Below: *Crew chiefs place auxiliary fuel tank under the wing of a P-51.*

Below: *Control Jeep directs a B-24 to the runway for take-off.*

Above: *Two American corporals keep radio contact with the control tower.*

Above: *Crew Chief Master Sergeant Roberts gives his signal to cut engines.*

between top US and British military personnel in London to determine future cooperation of the United States if it entered the war. It was agreed that Europe was the critical theater and US heavy bombers would be utilized jointly with the RAF Bomber Command to eliminate German war production and industrial centers. From the start a combined bomber offensive was envisaged.

The two years before the United States actually entered the war the RAF gave us some insight into unescorted daylight bombing missions. In three months the RAF lost 20 Wellington bombers. The Germans also suffered heavy losses in daylight missions over Britain in 1940. Both air forces turned to night bombing, which, because of the lack of bombing accuracy and navigational techniques, still kept losses at a very high level.

By the time war was declared most of the kinks were worked out, and modifications already accomplished. Now the setting was right and the next step was to send an advance force to England to prepare the way for the US air echelon.

More than 100 years after the Duke of Wellington remarked that the Battle of Waterloo had been won on the playing fields of Eton, victory in the greatest war in history was assured by an air force controlled and directed from the grounds of a distinguished girls grammar school.

From Wycombe Abbey, in Buckinghamshire, England, nestled in the foothills of the scenic Chilterns, the 8th United States Air Force conducted its

Below: *The famous* Memphis Belle *completed 25 missions on 9 June 1943.*

Numbered Air Forces

The expansion of the Air Corps resulted in its organizational structure being revised, especially above the group and wing levels. On 20 June 1941 the War Department established the United States Army Air Force with Major General Henry H Arnold as commander. This did wonders for the proper management and control of such a large force, and which would give birth in 1947 to the United States Air Force as a branch of the US Armed Forces. The following is a list of the Numbered Air Forces of the Army Air Force.

1st Air Force	Northeast US
2nd Air Force	Northwest US
3rd Air Force	Southeast US
4th Air Force	Southwest US
5th Air Force	Pacific
6th Air Force	Panama Canal
7th Air Force	Pacific
8th Air Force	England
9th Air Force	North Africa/England
10th Air Force	India
11th Air Force	Alaska
12th Air Force	North Africa/Italy/England
13th Air Force	Pacific
14th Air Force	China
15th Air Force	Italy
20th Air Force	Pacific

Above: *Crew chief assists pilot of a P-47 prior to take-off from an 8th Air Force base in England.*

three-year campaign to destroy the industrial heart of Nazi Germany. This sustained assault began on 4 July 1942, when six crews of the 15th Bombardment Squadron (Light), utilizing borrowed Royal Air Force A-20 Douglas Boston III bombers from No 226 Squadron, made a token raid against Luftwaffe installations in Holland.

The Bostons ran into very heavy anti-aircraft fire, and two 8th Air Force planes were lost, but the raid saw the birth of USAAF daylight bombing experiences which were to prove invaluable in future strikes.

This 4 July sortie provided strong evidence of the A-20's capacity for absorbing punishment. One of the US-operated Bostons, piloted by Captain Charles C Kegelman, CO, suffered severe wing damage, lost its starboard airscrew from flak and had an engine fire. It was thought to have crashed near its objective, but the pilot somehow managed to bring it back to Swanton Morley on the one remaining engine, shooting up an enemy flak tower on the return flight. This aircraft type was to fly a total of 39,492 sorties and drop 31,856 tons of bombs while assigned to the European Theater. It was adaptable, reliable and potent. It must be ranked high among the US aircraft industry's exceptional combat aircraft designs utilized during the war.

Below: *Six 0.50 caliber machine guns plus ammunition are loaded onto a P-51 Mustang Fighter.*

Top center: *WACS stride down the apron of Maxwell Field, Alabama prior to their assignment with the 8th Air Force.*
Top right: *Lead pilot gives some pointers to bombardiers of the 8th Air Force.*
Above: *Boeing B-17s as seen by an Me-109 over Germany.*
Below: *B-17s in a practice flight over the English countryside.*

Above: *Ground crew change an engine.* Below: *US 8th AF bases in East Anglia on 15 October 1943.*

From this minute beginning grew the air force which, during the last year of the war in Europe, sent an average of 1200 bombers thundering into the Third Reich, and dropped an average of one ton of bombs for every minute of that year.

Under the overall command and direction of General Carl A Spaatz, and the control of First Lt General Ira C Eaker, and later Lt General Jimmy H Doolittle, the wartime 8th Air Force grew to a force of 200,000 men, which by Christmas Eve 1944, was able to send 2000 bombers, 1000 fighters and 21,000 airmen into the air over enemy territory in a single mission.

Dispatched from the Top Secret underground-complex, codenamed Pinetree, the mighty armadas of the 8th devastated Hitler's Europe with 700,000 tons of bombs, 530,000 tons of which were dropped on targets inside Germany.

The 8th spewed onto enemy industries and military installations a total of 4,375,984 high explosive, fragmentation and large incendiary devices ranging from 500lbs to 2000lbs each. In addition, it dropped 27,556,978 small, four-pound incendiary bombs.

By itself, the 8th Air Force was responsible for about 32 percent of the entire strategic air effort throughout the war against Germany. This offensive brought on a near-complete economic collapse, resulted in the destruction of the Luftwaffe, laid waste to key industries, devastated 61 major cities, disrupted the entire enemy transportation systems and left Hitler's armies demoralized and isolated on the battlefields. Altogether 2,689,000 tons of bombs were dropped by the 8th Air Force, its sister air forces and the Royal Air Force.

Of the 242 airfields built by the British Government for the United States Army Air Force, 50 percent were eventually occupied by the 8th Air Force. These airfields cost the British taxpayer in excess of $600 million. Besides the airfields there were

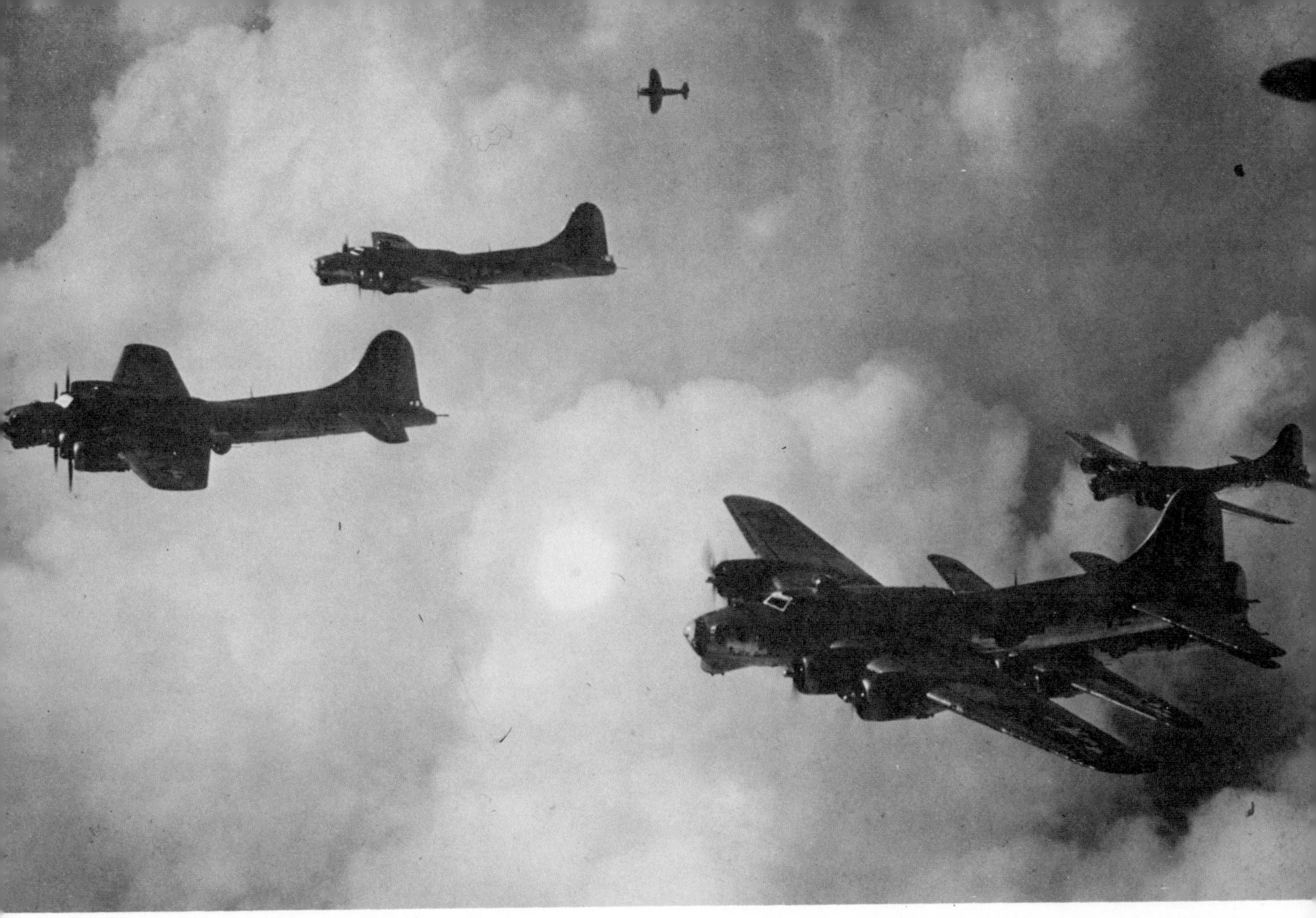

numerous other stations: crew replacement centers, gunnery schools, quartermaster's depots and repair units. The most important locations were the Combat Wings HQ, the majority established in stately British homes: Brampton Grange, Elvedon Hall and Ketteringham Hall to name a few. The actual airfields were usually named after the nearest hamlet or village: Attlebridge, Alconbury, Bassingbourne, Bovingdon, Bungay, Chelveston, Deenethorpe, Duxford, Deopham Green, Seething, Sculthorpe, Wendling and Wattisham.

The first real involvement of the United States Army Air Force in the European Theater occurred when the first operational B-17E arrived in the United Kingdom. The B-17E was specifically designed for offensive strategic operations; it had incorporated within its framework, major changes which improved its bombing stability and introduced defenses which made it the most protected aircraft in the world. It arrived on 20 May 1942, and was assigned to the 97th Bombardment Group (Heavy), Polebrook, England. Major General Dwight D Eisenhower flew to England for a tour of the country during May and was greeted by 'Goode Olde English Fog.' The fog delayed his tour for over 48 hours; upon arriving Eisenhower was introduced to a young woman who was to make quite an impression on his life, his future driver and secretary Kay Summersby. In fact, Kay introduced him to his first English pub, in Beaconsfield, The Royal Standard of England. Its claim to fame was that it was the 'Oldest Pub in England'. Kay also introduced him to other aspects of English life and helped further to forge Anglo-American relations.

After many political, strategic and tactical arguments, in August 1942 strategic operations were finally agreed on between the 8th Air Force and the Royal Air Force for a coordinated day and night nonstop offensive. The 17 August 1942 saw General Ira C Eaker

Above: *A P-51 of the 8th Air Force hovers near a formation of B-17s over England.*

Below: *English girls watch air mechanics work on B-24 engines.*

Below: *B-17s line up ready to make strategic bombing raids on Germany.*

in *Yankee Doodle* (41-9023) lead 12 B-17Es, 97th Bombardment Group (H) against the marshaling yards at Rouen-Sotteville, in France, while a further six aircraft flew a diversionary strike. This formation was escorted by RAF Spitfires and sustained no losses.

Ira C Eaker, the Commander of the 8th Air Force in England, was one of the major proponents of the strategic bombing concept and had been one of Billy Mitchell's supporters. He had been a school teacher prior to applying for a commission in August 1917. He served with the 2nd and 3rd Air Squadrons, Philippines, 1919–22 and upon returning to the United States assumed command of the 5th Air Squadron, at Mitchell Field, New York, 1922–23. From 1923–32 he served in executive office positions in Washington DC. He commanded the 34th Pursuit Squadron, 17th Pursuit Group in 1935 and then returned to Washington to an air staff position from 1938–40. He then moved on to

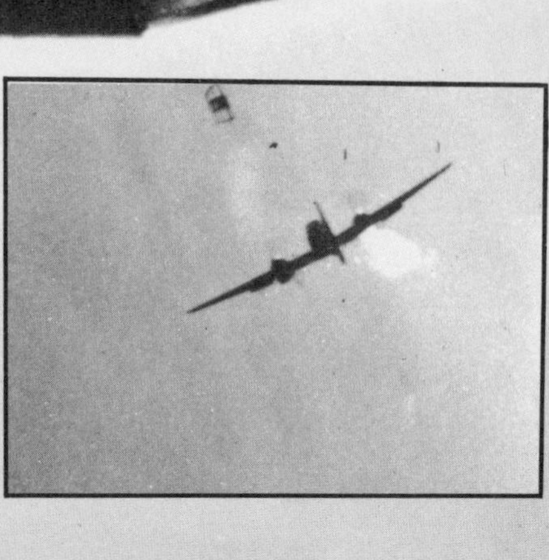

Above: *Formation of Douglas A-24s.*
Right and Far right: *Twin-engined German aircraft being shot down by Lt Richard A Stearns on 5 November 1943.*

Left: *Alexander Bogmolov presents the Order of Kutuzov, Russia's highest military award, to Lt Gen Ira C Eaker.*
Far left: *Crew of* Wash's Tub, *a Consolidated B-24.*

Below: *Capt Charles S Hudson, bombardier, in the nose of his plane.*

B-17E

Fuselage: 73ft 10in
Weight empty: 32,250lbs
Weight combat: 51,000lbs
Fuel capacity: 1730gal
Max fuel capacity: 2520gal
Max range: 2000 miles at 25,000ft
Max speed: 317mph at 25,000ft
Initial climb: 1100ft/min
Crew: 10 men
Armament: 8 × 0.50in
1 × 0.30in

Above: *Officers of the 381st Bomb Group enjoy their Thanksgiving Dinner 1943 at Ridgewell, Essex.*

command the 20th Fighter Group, Hamilton Field, California, from January–September 1941, and was shortly sent to the United Kingdom as a Special Observer. He was assigned to the 1st AF headquarters, Mitchell Field, November 1941, and was handpicked to lead an expeditionary bomber command to the United Kingdom. He arrived in February 1942 with staff and assumed command of 8th Bomber Command. He was an officer of experience, reliability and gifted with enough foresight to see the need for a strong daylight bombing force.

Below: *A mechanic runs a patch through top turret guns of a B-17.*

All was not easy in England as a technician stationed at High Wycombe, HQ 8th Bomber Command, remembered when over 350 new personnel arrived at the camp. They had a two-mile hike up Daws Hill and had a bowl of mutton stew for their reward. Their quarters consisted of pup tents under the heavy foliage. The men had to use their topcoats as mattresses and to make matters worse, the rains came and the tents leaked like sieves. All in all, it was a memorable welcome to a place called Wycombe. The last phrase that first night was 'war sure is hell.' The British standing comment about American GIs is still remembered today, 'they were overpaid, overfed, oversexed and over here.' The US reply was the British men were 'underpaid, underfed, undersexed and under Eisenhower.'

Above: *This engine from a B-17 is to be replaced by a reconditioned one.*

The initial success of the first bombing mission of 17 August renewed the faith of the United States Army Air Force Commanders in high-level precision bombing. On 18 August the 326th Bombardment Squadron arrived at Prestwick, Scotland with the much improved B-17F model, after a nonstop flight from Gander, Newfoundland. This was part of the 92nd Bombardment Group (H), which was destined to become the oldest group in the 8th Air Force, and had the privilege to lead the last bombing mission of the war. Now the 8th was assured of three operational heavy bomb groups: the 92nd Bomb Group at Bovingdon, 97th Bomb Group at Polebrook and the 301st Bomb Group at Chelveston; and four fighter groups: the 14th FGp at Atcham with P-38s, 1st FGp at Ibsley with P-38Fs, 31st FGp at Westhamnett with Spitfire Vs and the 52nd FGp at Goxhill with Spitfire Vs, and the 15th Bombardment Squadron (L) at Molesworth with Boston IIIs.

With this force, Spaatz now had the firm foundation of a strategic force on which to build. But this was destined to be short-lived, due to the Allied invasion of North Africa. The 8th was asked to supply the nucleus for the air elements of the new 9th and 12th Air Forces. The 12th was to be commanded by none other than Brigadier General Jimmy H Doolittle who was currently commanding the 4th Bombardment Wing.

The North African campaign had priority over men and equipment go-

Top right: *P-51s form up as they climb for altitude.*
Right: *White-nosed P-51 of the 8th Air Force over England.*

WR
P

B-17F
Fuselage: 74ft 9in
Weight empty: 34,000lbs
Weight combat: 56,500lbs
Fuel capacity: 1730 US gallons
Max fuel capacity: 3630 US gallons
Max range: 2000 miles at 25,000ft
Max speed: 300mph at 25,000ft
Initial climb: 1115ft/min
Armament: 11 ×.50in
Crew: Ten men

Right: *B-17s in formation over England on another bombing mission.* Below: *Lt Vernon L Richards at the controls of his North American P-51 over England.*

ing to the 8th but also pressure from the CINCUS was demanding support for the Pacific Theater where air support was drastically needed by MacArthur. Spaatz and Eaker were determined to get as much experience as possible for their Bomber Command before losing its original two B-17 groups.

The mission of most importance in the fall of 1942 was against the steel and engineering works of the *Compagnie de Fives* in Belgium, and the locomotive and freight car works of the *Ateliers d'Hellemmes* both at Lille on 9 October. One hundred and fifteen heavy bombers were dispatched, including seven on a diversionary sortie. They encountered the stiffest opposition to date of the war. The 97th and 301st were the main attack groups plus small elements of the 92nd, and the 93rd and 306th were on their initial combat missions. The B-24s of the 93rd were ordered to bring up the rear of the formation. The escort force for this mission was quite substantial; a heavy force of Royal Air Force Spitfires and USAAF fighters rendezvoused with the main force in mid-channel, but Luftwaffe orders were to avoid the escort and eliminate the bomber force.

Left: *Pilot and co-pilot Lts Bob Boundrecor and Ned Hawkins in their B-17.*

Bottom: *An early example of telephone booth crowding by two 8th Air Force crewmen in England.*

Left: *British children at an Easter party given by the 391st Bomb Group in 1944.*

The 93rd and 306th had poor bombing patterns resulting in many civilian casualties outside the target areas. The losses for the day were three B-17s lost and one B-24, while the Germans lost, according to revised statistics published by 8th Bomber Command, 21-21-15, but this figure is still too high, if German figures are accurate.

The poor performance of the B-24 Liberators was a matter of note on this their first operational bombing mission. Out of 24, ten reached the target and 14 turned back due to various mechanical and personnel failures. The B-24 nose turrets restricted the outlook of the bombardier giving poor forward visibility which resulted in poor bombing patterns. Also the increased weight adversely affected the flying qualities of the aircraft when flown with maximum bomb loads. Stability was poor at high altitudes and perseverance was required to pilot a B-24. In these conditions, a B-24 was more likely not to survive battle damage than a B-17.

Although only four aircraft were lost on the mission, 36 B-17s and ten B-24s were damaged and this placed an immense burden on the repair crews to make these aircraft operational. The weather was bad during October but on the 21st the only other attack of the month was launched. The target was Lorient, the submarine base which, according to policy directives, was top priority due to the damage inflicted by the German U-Boats based there on the Atlantic convoys.

Sixty-six B-17s were dispatched from four heavy bombardment groups but only the 97th reached the target. The rest turned back because of heavy clouds which obscured the objective. The 97th thought it was their lucky day when a heaven-sent cloudbreak appeared from out of the blue; immediately dropping to 17,000ft they prepared for a bombing run on the target. Ironically, their luck ran out as fast as it came, they were hit from all sides by FW 190s as they crossed the coast. This attack all but eliminated the rear echelon of the formation. Three B-17s were shot down and six more severely damaged. The remaining fifteen B-17s managed to place 70 percent of their ordnance on target. Intelligence reported heavy damage to dock equipment and machinery, but only minimum damage to the actual submarine pens.

The 97th returned to England with

Left: Sgt M J Barraza, gunner and radio operator mans the waist gun of a B-17

Above: *B-17s practice the box formation over England.*
Above right: *Master Sergeant J P Wellmaker cleans the 50-caliber guns of a B-17 as an English farmer's wife herds her ducks away from the plane.*
Below: *Exhausted crew of a Consolidated B-24 after their return to England from a bombing raid over Germany.*

Above: *Members of a B-17 crew, left to right: ball turret gunner, tail gunner, left waist gunner, right waist gunner, engineer, radio operator, co-pilot, bombardier and pilot.*

the highest loss of any bomber group to that date and with a very healthy respect for the Luftwaffe fighter pilots. This turned out to be the 97th's last mission with the 8th Air Force, as the group received orders to start deploying to North Africa on 9 November and the 301st followed on 26 November.

From November 1942 to May 1943 the USAAF strategic bombing offensive was conducted by four B-17 groups: the 91st at Bassingbourne, 306th at Thurleigh, 303rd at Molesworth and 305th at Chelveston; and two B-24 groups: the 93rd at Hardwick and the 44th at Shipdam.

During this period Spaatz assumed command of the US African Air Forces, and Eaker was left to hold the fort back in England. The winter of 1942–43 was hard, to say the least, and as far as the 8th was concerned, operational losses far outstripped replacements.

The North African campaign continued to bleed the 8th of valuable equipment and machines. But what was worse, the 93rd was redeployed to the 9th Air Force and 12th Air Force through late March 1943, and two badly needed B-17 groups programmed for the United Kingdom were sent to Africa.

> In addition to four fighter and two heavy bomber groups, the Eighth Air Force had turned over trained personnel to the extent of 3,198 officers, 34 warrant officers and 24,124 enlisted men, of whom 1,098 officers, 7,101 enlisted men and 14 warrant officers came from Eighth Bomber Command alone. The remaining heavy bombardment groups (44th, 91st, 92nd, 93rd, 303rd, 304th and 305th) suffered considerably from loss of such essential equipment as bomb-loading appliances and transport vehicles. They suffered even more from complete lack of replacement of both crews and aircraft, a fact which made it impossible to keep a large force in the air even when weather conditions permitted.

The above quote reveals that the 8th Air Force was practically grounded until May 1943, first by demands of the North African campaign and secondly by a winter of great severity.

On 3 January 1943 the first mission of the new year was planned, target St Nazaire (Flak City). Brigadier General Haywood Hansell flew as an observer with the 85-plane bomber force to check out the effectiveness of Colonel Curtis LeMay's revolutionary new air tactics. The idea was to make a straight long run-in at 20,000ft for optimum bomb results. Visibility was outstanding and the absence of clouds was notable, but with all good things come the bad, in this specific case, a sub-stratospheric storm which doubled the time of the initial bombing run. The German anti-aircraft (AA) batteries defending Flak City were able to lay a barrage of intense AA fire into the paths of the on-coming bombers. The barrage lasted for over ten minutes and was one of the most intense and accurate of the entire war.

Three B-17s were lost to the flak, four more to fighters and 47 aircraft sustained battle damage. To date, these were the heaviest losses endured by 8th Bomber Command. The 8th continued to polish and refine the art of daylight precision bombing, but the question still lingered about its true effectiveness and overall contribution to the strategic war effort.

After thirty missions, the key question to the overall scope of bomber operations was 'Could the USAAF bombers conduct vigorous and potent

Left: *Formation of 8th AF B-17s.*
Right: *Master Sergeant Harrell Farrah is seen through the engine cowling ring of a B-17 while repairing the engine of another peirod.*

Left: *Capt Don S Gentile entertains a guest at the officer's club.*
Below: *Major General E R Quesada, throws the first baseball.*
Below left: *Nine-year-old Norah Colgan of London is surrounded by 3564 candy bars, packets of cookies and chewing gum raised by USAAF.*

Above: *Men of the 401st Bomb Group at their PX (Post Exchange) in 1944.*
Below left: *June dance in 1943 given by the 381st Bomb Group.*
Bottom left: *Enlisted men's dance, like so many others, cemented Anglo-American relations.*
Below right: *Chat-up time during a lull in the dancing.*
Bottom right: *Bing Crosby entertained more than 4000 GIs and RAF personnel in one of his tours of US bases.*

strategic strikes without prohibitive losses?'

Strategic bombing results varied. The 8th was confronted with numerous problems when attempting to follow the US bombing doctrine. The greatest were weather conditions. Good visibility for daylight precision bombing was practically nonexistent from mid-December to early March. Clouds were a factor which had to be taken into account, for the average number of cloudless days during the winter of 1942–43 was two per month.

The winter weather on the ground also set back operations. The English weather was never very good, and had one thing which was a serious threat to operational efficiency of aircraft. Moisture and dampness which could seep into the functional parts of an aircraft, could freeze and turn to ice at very high altitudes. New anti-freeze oils were developed to solve problems such as turret and bomb-door mechanisms and trimming tabs freezing-up and superchargers failing because of oil congealing in regulator lines.

Other factors of major importance and influence on 8th Bomber Command's operations were the demands and necessary support required by the newly formed Air Forces, the 9th and 12th in North Africa. Required to train these units, the 8th lost 80 percent of its supplies and spare units to them.

But what was needed at this stage of the game was favorable publicity. The desire of the entire command from the Commander down to the lowest buck private was to attack Germany. The High Wycombe command complex gave first priority to the submarine yards, but uncommon interest was shown about Vegesack, located thirty miles from its North Sea estuary on the river Weser.

Below: *Sgt Arthur Dwyer works on the engine of a B-24.*

Against this target, on 27 January 1943, operational orders were issued. The attack was led by the oldest operational group in the command, the 306th Bombardment Group (H) with 64 B-17s. The man who was handpicked to lead this important mission was Colonel Frank Armstrong, former commander of the 97th, and now of the revitalized 306th. The route selected took them a considerable distance out over the North Sea to avoid being sighted by the enemy along the coast who could have telegraphed their destination. After climbing towards bombing altitude, weather conditions worsened and it became apparent that by the time the enemy coast was reached cloud formations inland would prohibit delivery. Armstrong undaunted, ordered the force to proceed towards its secondary target, the German port of Wilhelmshaven. At 1110 hours, the B-17s crossed the hostile shores of Germany for the first time in the war. Wilhelmshaven had cloud cover, but gaps allowed 58 B-17s to deliver their loads. Hindered by a smokescreen, the resulting damage was only minor. German opposition was noted to be highly ineffective. Losses amounted to two B-24s and one B-17, while the enemy fighter defense force lost at least seven aircraft.

The next raid was the rail marshaling yards at Hamm, in the heavily fortified Ruhr area and the next most important phase occurred in March 1943, when the North African campaign began to be phased out; the combat strength of the 8th increased as long sought-after replacements started rolling in from the States. Finally, the tide started turning in the 8th's favor with the arrival of four B-17 groups in April 1943, doubling its combat strength. Also in April, the 92nd at Bovingdon became an operational unit, flying the YB-40 gunships. The B-24 groups were raised to peak strength, and the 93rd returned from its loan to the 12th Air Force after 75 days. This gave Eaker a force of 500 operational bombers; things were finally beginning to take shape.

On 4 May, against the Ford and General Motors vehicle factories at Antwerp, Belgium, a milestone was reached when P-47 Thunderbolts completed their first escort bombing mission without one single loss. The 8th was now beginning to be successful, but to be successful, bombing results must be good and accurate. This was achieved through experience and superlative training techniques which were proven gradually by the number of direct hits within a target radius of 1000 meters. At the beginning the 8th's average was just under 15 percent, but by March 1943, it was up to 75 percent. The Royal Air Force photo reconnaissance missions proved beyond a doubt the accuracy of the air strikes. The only problem with estimated inflicted battle damage was, of course, being too optimistic.

The USAAF's daylight strategic bomber's ability to survive without fighter escort was sorely tested from May–October 1943. This period, although only six months long, was like fifty years to the airmen of the 8th who engaged the enemy in the most epic air battles of the war.

By mid-May the new groups were considered operational, and this provided Eaker with an opportunity to commit 221 bombers. On 14 May concrete evidence was witnessed that the pattern of bombing operations was changing. Eaker ordered 235 heavy and medium bombers to attack four separate targets. The 14 May saw the B-26 Martin Marauder committed to action for the first time during the war with the 8th Air Force.

The Martin B-26A Marauder entered service with the USAAF in 1941. It was initially given the title of 'Flying Torpedo' by the new media due to its perfect circular structural design. This initial accolade was changed very quickly by its pilots to 'Flying Prostitute' and the 'Widow Maker' and the epithets were unprintable.

The B-26 met with unprecedented success in the North Africa campaign, as a long range fighter. It had the high speed and long range to intercept the cumbersome German ME 323 and JU52/3M transports far out over the Mediterranean, and shoot them down in scores. But they met with less success as part of the 8th's medium bomber force.

The design of the original B-26 was submitted on 5 July 1939 to Brigadier General Fickel at Wright Field. It was based on the incorporation of two Pratt-Whitney R-2800 Double Warp eighteen cylinder radial engines each capable of 1850hp. This aircraft had one 0.3in machine gun mounted in the upper half of the symmetrical and frameless plastic nose, and a similar hand-operated gun in the tail section. The wings were shoulder-mounted and possessed no fillets. It was far ahead of its time, especially in displaying four-bladed airscrews with root cuffs to aid in engine cooling. It had two-speed mechanical superchargers to maintain engine power up to medium altitude, and ejector exhausts vented on each side of the nacelle.

Above right: *Backstage of a USO show in January 1944.*
Right: *Staff Sergeants Lammering and Wilbur Stewart work on a P-51.*

Right: *Lt. Clark Gable with two belts of machine gun ammunition at the Army Air Forces Flexible Gunnery School at Tyndall Field, Florida.*
Center: *Queen Elizabeth visits an 8th Air Force base to inspect the famous B-17* Memphis Belle.
Far right: *Commander Jack Dempsey of the US Coast Guard watches Corporal Billy Conn of the US Army Air Service Command (right) square off against Sergeant Freddie Mills, British light heavyweight champion, at a Special Service boxing show.*

The B-26 was the first USAAF aircraft to operate successfully at night, and acquired an excellent reputation for precision bombing strikes on bridges and railheads in France.

In support of the 14 May mission, the RAF committed light bombers and fighters which drew a substantial amount of German fighters away from the US heavies. The new groups were dispatched against Antwerp and Courtrai, to lure German fighters from the northern part of France and the Low Countries Defense Force, while the main strike force was dispatched against the submarine yards at Kiel. The B-26s attacked the Velson power stations at Ijmuiden in Holland. The bombing results were variable, and the losses would have been light, except that the unlucky 44th lost six B-24s from its rear echelon.

The B-26s' first mission resulted in heavy battle damage to themselves, and the mission was a complete failure as not a single bomb hit the target at Ijmuiden. A second strike was ordered on 17 May and it was a disaster. Eleven aircraft reached Holland, none returned; a major navigational error arose which put the entire flight over the extremely heavy flak defenses of the Maas Estuary resulting in its total destruction. This brought about the immediate assignment of the B-26s to 8th Air Force Air Support Command for tactical use only. It also stopped low level medium bomber attacks by the 8th.

Eighth Bomber Command plans were deceptive from the beginning of the campaign. They utilized one ploy after another, some successful, others disastrous. The German fighter inter-

Right: *Princess Elizabeth Christens* Rose of York, *a Flying Fortress named in her honor.*

ceptors only had about ninety minutes on internal fuel; therefore, once committed to one sector, they would lose their combat effectiveness in another. If Gruppen J.G. 11 was committed to Sector A and enemy bombers were picked up on radar in Sector B, the Gruppen would have to be recalled to base to refuel before being committed to Sector B. This was a tactical problem of which the 8th took full advantage at every opportunity. The bombers had 1,000 miles of coastline to choose from, forcing the Luftwaffe to disperse their units over a very wide front. Each mission became a tantalizing battle of wits between the German fighter controllers and the Allied bomber formations. The recognition of objectives and diversions made all the difference in whether bombing results were good and damage to the attacking force light. If the German fighter controllers recognized an objective in time, they would commit all their available fighters to the elimination of that specific bomber formation.

The new Fortress groups arriving in the United Kingdom were proving to have a more rigid standard of training. Under extreme pressure the USAAF had established a totally comprehensive training program conducted by two commands, Flying Training and Technical Training, which merged to become the Army Air Force Training Command in July 1943. Although the new B-17 groups were graduates of a more complete and exhausting training program, there was absolutely no substitute for the one essential factor – combat experience. These groups were definitely more proficient but didn't have the practical training allowed to the original groups. Now the Luftwaffe was putting up much more determined resistance as the Allied bombers advanced steadily into the territory of the Third Reich. The new groups learned the hard way. Poorly assembled bomber formations, lack of cohesive command control and failure to maintain correct distance resulted in severe losses. The 4th Bombardment Wing (H) discovered this to their horror, during the 13 June attack on Kiel, when 26 B-17s were destroyed: two were aircraft from the new groups. This was a definite blow to the Combined Bomber Offensive.

At this point, it is necessary to delve into the background of the 'Combined Bomber Offensive'. This directive was authorized at the Casablanca Conference in January but was not officially released until 10 June. The Combined Bomber Offensive (CBO) was the end product of an astute and careful analysis of the German war economy by a select strategic study group. Their findings resulted in the CBO plan priorities.

For the USAAF the Combined Bomber Offensive outlined the force required to eliminate Germany's war production capabilities and submitted the tentative date of 31 March 1944. The figure given was 51 bombardment groups composed of 2702 heavy bombers. But by June 1943 the revised number was 56 groups for a new total of 3054 heavies.

The actual build-up was given some priority at the time the Combined Bomber Offensive was established. In April 1943, the B-17 force grew from 200 to 300 operational aircraft. The arrival of additional groups in June and July raised the total to 600, but then a lull in deliveries occurred. The B-24 Liberator groups were deployed to North Africa during this critical period, leaving nine B-17 groups of the 1st Bombardment Wing and seven of the 4th to carry out the US contribution. The future size of the 8th Bomber Command was to have been 75 percent of the entire USAAF heavy bomber groups. To insure the effective and efficient operational management and direction of what otherwise would have been an unwieldy outfit, the plan was to establish four bombardment divisions. This new bombardment division idea was the forerunner of the modern USAF air division. In actual fact, the change was only numerical and entailed a minor paperwork alteration – 1st Bombardment Wing to 1st Bombardment Division. The change became effective in September.

The most successful operation in June was a strike against an important synthetic rubber factory in the Ruhr. Two hundred and thirty-five B-17s were dispatched and 75 percent of these actually bombed the target. The result was excellent, the damage put the plant out of action for over a month. The ironic fact behind this was that the target fell into the secondary target position of the Combined Bomber Offensive plan; consequently no follow-up strikes were launched. This allowed the Germans to have the plant back in full operation by the end of the year. The weather for the rest of June was extremely bad delaying any planned deep strikes into Germany.

The next 8th Air Force offensive became known as 'Blitz Week'. Eaker seeing a golden opportunity created by clear, blue skies, launched his bombers in all directions. On 24 July, 324 B-17s were heading out over the North Sea toward various targets. The 1st Bombardment Wing's destination was Heroya over 1900 miles roundtrip for a strike against a brand new nitrate factory. Due to its extra fuel capacity, the 4th was assigned to hit Bergen and Trondheim harbors, 960 miles away. One hundred and sixty-seven B-17s stopped nitrate production until November, and wreaked havoc on the nearby uncompleted aluminum and magnesium plants. One Fortress *Georgia Rebel,* 381st Bombardment Group (H), was crippled by flak but managed to limp into neutral Sweden. The 4th Bombardment Wing had a fine day at Trondheim, but the Bergen run had to return with their ordinance, as the target area was clouded over. Opposition to this strike was light, the Luftwaffe was apparently taken off-guard by the change of tactics.

The 25 July saw the 1st Bombardment Wing head for Kiel, a section to Hamburg and the 4th Bombardment Wing to Warnemünde. The Kiel groups fulfilled their strike but cloud conditions forced the other groups to seek alternative targets. Although a huge pall of smoke was present over Hamburg from the Royal Air Force's night raid, the Forts managed to drop their ordinance prior to the clouds settling-in. The cost was high though, nineteen B-17s were lost.

Eighth Bomber Command was starting to record heavy losses but undaunted, 300 bombers were dispatched 24 hours later. The pressure was beginning to build up. It was one thing for a 21-year-old pilot to be sipping a pint of English beer, at a local pub, away from the real war. But in this young pilot's heart he knew in 8 hours he would be piloting an aircraft through hell itself. Flak breaking all around, ME 109s and FW 190s closing in from all angles – yet it was in this young airman that the fighting spirit was kindled to combat a force which was attempting to dominate the world.

The men and machines of the 8th struck at Hamburg and Hannover with two combat wings on 26 July. The 92 B-17s which hit the Hannover Continental Gummi Werke, a synthetic rubber plant of critical value to the German war effort, met with resounding success. The plant took over 21 direct hits and cut back production by over 25 percent for several months afterwards.

The remainder of July saw Eaker's 8th Bomber Command continuously attack such targets as Oschersleben, Kassel, Hamburg and Hannover. Blitz Week was marked by the most furious air battles of the war. The Luftwaffe lost over 40 fighters, the Allies 128 B-17s; the ratio was roughly 1 to 3.

The 8th had a well-earned two week rest which allowed the air staff to come up with the most ambitious strike ever planned. The neutralization and eventual elimination of Luftwaffe opposition was still a primary objective and the destruction of fighter production facilities was the nucleus of the plan. Regensburg and Wiener Neustadt

were the main production centers for the ME 109s but the tactical problem involved in striking both these targets was the distance. In both cases it meant putting the attacking formations under constant enemy fighter pressure for hours with an estimated loss of 60 percent. A tactical ploy was planned to alleviate partially some of the enemy fighter force. The B-17s would hit the target and proceed over the Alps directly to Allied installations in North Africa. German controllers would have scrambled their air cover to hit the returning B-17s, who would not be returning at all but proceeding in a southeasterly direction. The 9th Air Force's two B-24 groups and three B-17 groups would attack Wiener Neustadt from North Africa. The 8th would attack Regensburg and Schweinfurt – two names which the men of the 8th would never forget. The initial date was set for 7 August but as usual once again bad weather delayed the strike. The 9th Air Force's B-24 Liberators attacked on the 13 August when the opportunity presented itself but the 8th was still delayed. However, missions were still continuously flown against German industry in the Ruhr to maintain the pressure.

Finally, the weather broke on 17 August, the anniversary of 8th Bomber Command's first operational sortie from England, and the Schweinfurt mission had the green light at last. The 4th Bombardment Wing was given the order to attack Regensburg while the 1st Bombardment Wing struck at Schweinfurt and its ball-bearing factories. A major battle was predicted due to the great distances involved and the importance of targets to the German war effort.

A dawn take-off was planned but

Above: *Practice flight of the 8th Air Force's Flying Fortresses (Boeing B-17s) over the English countryside.*

Below: *Cargo is loaded into a Douglas C-47, workhorse of the USAAF and counterpart to Germany's JU52.*

Aircraft names of note

ALL HELL	F-47C	61FS/56FG
ASCEND CHARLIE	B-17F	571BS/390BG
ANGEL'S PLAYMATE	P-51D	354FG
ARKANSAS TRAVELER	B-24D	98BG
BAD EGG	B-17F	401BS/91BG
BAD PENNY	B-17F	322BS/91BG
BAG O' BOLTS	B-24H	715BS/448BG
BANSHEE	B-26B	387BG
BATTLE AX	P-61	425NFS
BOCK'S BOCKSCAR	B-29	393BS(VH)/ 509CG/ 315BW Nagasaki
BETTY AND JIM	B-24H	847BS/489BG
BIG BEAUTIFUL DOLL	P-51D	84FS/78FG
BIRMINGHAM BLITZKRIEG	B-17E	414BS/379BG
BLACK BARNEY	P-38J	77FS/20FG
BOEING'S BEST	B-17G	365BS/305BG
BUNNY'S HONEY	B-26B	344BG
BOMBOOGIE	B-17F	401BS/91BG
BOOMERANG	B-24D	328BS/93BG
BOOM TOWN	B-17F	305BG
BUGS BUNNY	B-17G	390BG
BUTCHER SHOP	B-17E	340BS/97BG
CALAMITY JANE	B-17F	390BG
CANNON BALL	B-17F	511BS/351BG
CAREFUL VIRGIN	B-17F	323BS/91BG
CAROLINA QUEEN	B-17G	381BG
CARTER'S LITTLE LIVER PILLS	B-17F	364BS/305BG
CHENNAULTS PAPPY	B-17F	306BG
CLASSY CHASSY	B-24H	487BG
CONTRARY MARY	P-51	84FS/78FG
COOKIE	P-47	351FS/353FG
CRIME DOCTOR	B-26	386BG
DADDY'S GIRL	P-51D	370FS/359FG
DANGEROUS DAN	B-17F	524BS/379BG
DESERT VAGABOND JR	B-25C	12BG
DEVIL'S OWN	B-17G	493BG
DINAH MIGHT	B-17G	493BG
DOUBLE LUCKY	P-47D	61FS/56FG
DOUBLE TROUBLE	B-26C	323BG
DOVE OF PEACE	P-51D	353FG
THE DUCHESS	B-17F	359BS/303BG
EASY ACES	B-17F	94BG
EASY ANGELS	P-47D	23FS/36FG
EIGHT BALL	B-17F	511BS/351BG
ENOLA GAY	B-29	393BS(VH)/ 509CG/ 315BW Hiroshima
EXCALIBUR	B-17F	91BG
FANCY NANCY	B-17F	612BS/401BG
FIREBALL	B-17F	351BG
FLAK BAIT	B-26B	449BS/322BG
FLAK DODGER	B-17G	750BS/457BG
FLAK HAPPY	B-26B	452BS/322BG
FLYING BISON	B-17G	427BS/303BG
FOULBALL	B-24H	490BG
FRISKIE	P-51C	381FS/363FG
GENERAL IKE	B-17G	401BS/91BG
GEORGIA REBEL	B-17F	535BS/381BG
GERONIMO	B-24D	93BG
GI WIFE	B-24J	487BG
GLORY BEE	B-24H	506BS/44BG
GREENWICH	B-24H	67BS/44BG
GREMLINS SWEETHEART	B-17F	95BG
GRIM RIP	P-40F	57FG

Below: *Crew of the* Memphis Belle *back from their 25th and final mission. Every crew member earned the DFC and Air Medal with three oak leaf clusters, and all survived with only one casualty, a leg wound to the tail gunner.*

HAIL COLUMBIA	B-24H	44BG
HALF PINT	P-47C	56FG
HELL'S ANGELS	B-17F	303BG
HELL'S ANGELS	B-26B	386BG
HELL'S BELL	B-26B	555BS/386BG
HELL'S FURY	B-26B	555BS/386BG
HELEN	A-20K	410BG
HIGHBALL	B-17F	511BS/351BG
HONEY BUN III	C-47	80TCS
HONEY CHILE	B-26B	554BS/386BG
HUN HUNTER FROM TEXAS	P-51D	355FG
HUN FLUSHER	F-6B	12TRS
HURRY HOME HONEY	P-51D	357FG
HUSLIN HUSSY	P-61	422NFS
I'LL BE AROUND	B-17G	95BG
IN THE MOOD	P-47D	56FG
INCENDIARY MARY	B-26B	386BG
IZA VAILABLE	B-17F	360BS/303BG
JACK THE RIPPER	B-17F	324BS/91BG
JAMAICA GINGER	B-17G	563BS/388BG
JERSEY BOUNCE	B-17F	358BS/303BG
JERSEY BOUNCE JR	B-17F	358BS/303BG
JIM DANDY	A-26	416BS
JOAN OF ARC	B-17F	369BS/306BG
JOE BTFSPLK	B-17F	427BS/303BG
JUST LAZY	P-38J	394FS/367FG
JOURNEY'S END	P-38J	38FS/55FG
KING BEE	B-26B	558BS/387BG
KNOCKOUT DROP	B-17F	559BS/303BG
LADY FAIRWEATHER	B-17F	359BS/303BG
LADY JANET	B-17G	729BS/452BG
LEADING LADY	B-17G	364BS/305BG
LEMON DROP	B-24D	68BS/44BG
LINDA BALL	B-17F	511BS/351BG
LITTLE AUDREY	B-17F	306BG
LITTLE BEAVER	B-24D	67BS/44BG
LITTLE BILL	P-47D	397FS/368FG
LITTLE DEMON	P-47D	351FS/353FG
LOVELY LADY	P-61	425NFS
MARY LU	B-26	324BG
MAGGIES DRAWERS	P-51B	363FG
MAGIC CARPET	P-47D	366FG
MRS WABBIL IV	P-51D	402FS/370FG
PATTY	P-47D	356FG
PEG O' MY HEART	P-51D	355FS
POON TANG	B-25C	340BG
RUTH	A-20	646BS
SANDRA ANN	B-26G	322BG
SECTION 8	F-6	109TRS
SPEED DEMON	P-47D	358FG
SHILLELAGH	P-51	354FG
SHADOW	P-47	391FS/366FG
SNOW WHITE AND THE SEVEN DWARVES	B-24D	98BG
THE FEATHER	B-26B	416BG
THE REAL McCOY	A-20	410BG
THE PRODIGAL SON	P-51D	356FS/354FG
THE SQUAW	B-24D	98BG
THE GREAT ARTISTE	B-29	393BS(VH)/509CG/315BW
THE WITCH	B-24D	543BS/98BG
WITCH HAZEL	C-47	314TCG

A-20 Douglas Havoc
Length: 48ft
Height: 17ft 7in
Wing area: 465sq ft
Span: 61ft 4in
Weight empty: 17,200lbs
Max combat load: 24,000lbs
Max speed: 317mph at 10,000ft
Max overload: 30,000lbs
Armament: 6 ×0.5in Colt-Browning machine guns in fixed nose positions with 350rpg; two 0.5in machine guns with 400rpg in a Martin power-operated dorsal turret and one 0.5in gun in a ventral tunnel.
Engines: Two Wright, R-2600-23, double cyclone, fourteen cylinder radial air-cooled engines with two-speed superchargers and driving 11ft 3in diameter, three blade Hamilton Standard Hydromatic airscrews. Each engine rated at 1600hp for take off and 1675hp for emergency conditions.

early fog and mist impeded visibility and the strike was delayed. In fact, at this stage of the game, it looked as if the entire mission would be scrubbed, but eventually the weather cleared and the seven B-17 groups of the 4th took off.

The 1st Bombardment Wing was still on the ground as the fog was thicker inland. This posed a tactical problem as all four P-47 Thunderbolt groups were committed to provide maximum protection for the bombers of the 4th. This chance to totally confuse and elude the enemy fighters was now lost.

At 1000hrs the 4th crossed the Dutch coast. They were led by Colonel Curtis E LeMay, the Wing Commander, who was flying with the 96th Bombardment Group from Snetterton Heath. The remaining groups were the 388th and 390th flying low and high respectively. LeMay, vigilant as ever, observed the groups had too much distance between them and ordered all units to close up. Castle's 94th Bombardment Group from Bury St Edmunds led the next combat wing with the 385th in the low position. The 95th Group had the lead in the last formation and the 100th Group from Thorpe Abbots the low; this last formation was carrying incendiaries.

The B-17s were supposed to have been escorted by two P-47 groups as far as the German border, but only one group actually did; the other group made a time miscalculation and turned back for base early. This left the entire rear echelon unprotected. The German fighters did not ignore opportunities such as this; 20 miles southeast of Brussels, FW 190s attacked the low squadrons of the low groups. Immediately two bombers of the 100th were shot down, and a further B-17 of the 95th dropped out of the formation. The FW190s were making mincemeat of the low squadrons and to make matters worse, the last P-47 group had to return as fuel reserves were extremely low. This left the bomber formation with absolutely no fighter cover. The B-17s continued on their course into Germany, meeting intense opposition all the way. The 'Bloody Hundredth' was the prime object of the Luftwaffe's main effort. The crew were staring with certainty into the inevitable face of death. For nearly 150 miles, FW 190s and ME 109s continuously attacked the last combat wing of the formation with a vengeance never before experienced by members of the 8th Air Force. Lt Colonel B Lay, an observer in one Fort, *Piccadilly Lily* thought 'the sight was fantastic'; he never forgot the picture of the ever-chasing enemy fighters attempting to annihilate the bomber force. As the formation sighted Mannheim, the attack changed from single-engine fighters to twin-engine ME 110 Zerstorers and JU 88 night fighters. Finally, just minutes before the target was reached, opposition ceased. This was more unnerving than the actual battle. In 90 minutes, seventeen B-17s had been shot down, thirteen of which were from the rear combat wing, and only five enemy fighters had been destroyed. However, bombing results at Regensburg were excellent; the objective was badly damaged, and unknown at the time, the fuselage jigs for the ME 262, the top secret German jet fighter were destroyed. This set back the estimated production date for months.

LeMay's bomber force encountered stiff opposition for approximately 30 minutes after completion of the last bombing run. But the Germans were taken completely by surprise when the formation turned southwest on a new heading, and they were really more occupied with an even greater mission which they saw beginning to develop.

This was the Schweinfurt raid against the ball-bearing production factories. The strike consisted of 230 B-17s, in four combat wings, commanded by Brigadier General R B Williams, who was flying with the 91st Bombardment Group. The 91st was the lead group and the 381st was in the low position. This formation followed the same route as the 4th Bombardment Wing but turned northeast at Mannheim.

From Schweinfurt came 50 percent of Germany's production of ball bearings, the critical component of so much that moves and vital to the production of aircraft and their engines. This raid was to have been the decisive thrust against the German aircraft industry and its production of single-engined front-line fighters which had more than doubled in the last nine months. The Luftwaffe committed 95 percent of its western fighter defense force, including J.G. 1 and J.G. 11 from the North German coast slightly over 250 miles away. Wave after wave of fighters converged upon the bomber force from all directions: Berlin, Hamburg, Holland, Belgium, northeastern France, Munich and Paris. Over 200 enemy fighters attacked the Schweinfurt formation reversing the tactics utilized earlier. They put their entire weight against the lead groups.

The bombing results were not as accurate as Regensburg but good despite the intense enemy fighter concentration. The losses sustained by the 1st Bomb Wing were very heavy; 36 B-17s and 374 airmen were lost. The 91st and 381st Bomb Groups were the hardest hit, and lost two-thirds of the final tally alone.

The Schweinfurt raid did accomplish one thing: the speedy delivery of P-51B Mustangs to the 8th Fighter Command. Originally, it was planned that only 180 P-51s were to be sent to the UK. Sixteen days after the Schweinfurt slaughter, General Henry H Arnold, ordered that the P-38s and P-51s were to have priority for a long-range fighter role with the 8th. If nothing else was learned from Schweinfurt, the very real need for fighter cover for a bombing force was unequivocally realized. A crash program was instituted by North American Aviation Inc to mass produce the Mustang in sufficient quantities to meet the 8th's need.

The P-51B could do 450mph at 30,000ft. It could outrun the FW 190 by 50mph at 28,000ft and 70mph

Right: *These three airmen brought the B-17* Reluctant Dragon *back safely from an air raid over Berlin after six crewmen bailed out and one gunner was killed.*
Below right: *Technical Sergeant Robert J Hanson kisses the ground after completing his 25th mission in the* Memphis Belle.
Below: *Damaged rudder of a B-17.*

above that. It was faster than ME 109 at all heights. It could out-dive and out-turn both German fighters. The Mustang was particularly suitable for long-range fighting by the addition of 'droppable' wings and belly gas tanks. This enabled the pilot to proceed on bomber escort to the farthest combat sector, then dropping them he became an interceptor fighter to which there was no equal. The P-51B made its first operational sortie with the 8th Fighter Command on 5 December 1943.

Schweinfurt could be looked upon as the turning point in the air war over Germany. Its result was the development and rapid production of the P-51B, the answer to long-range fighter cover which had previously been lacking. Now with adequate protection 8th Bomber Command was to strike at targets throughout Germany at will. After Regensburg and Schweinfurt, the winter weather set in and caused a lull in further strategic bombing operations.

Below: *Three North American P-51 Mustangs of the 13th Air Force.*

The Southern Flank

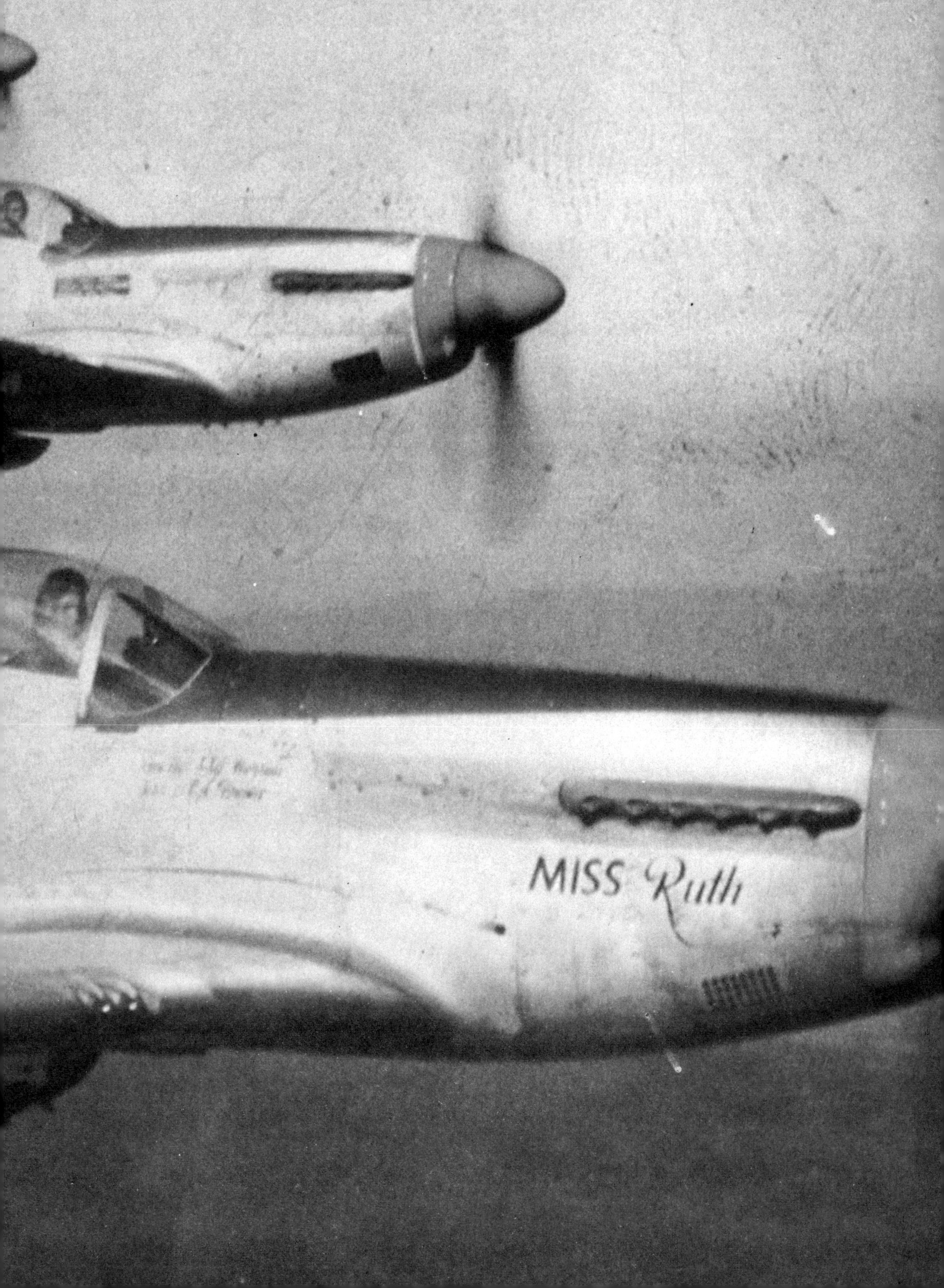

The invasion of North Africa was a political decision undertaken by Roosevelt for purely political reasons. A cross-channel invasion in the spring of 1943 was the quickest way to victory and Roosevelt could not afford a delay because if the Russians made a separate peace the Germans would practically be unbeatable, and the Allies were not ready for a second front in Europe at this time. A compromise was reached – Operation Torch, the invasion of North Africa.

The decision to invade North Africa, precluded the establishment of a second front in Europe in 1943 and to make matters worse, Roosevelt and Churchill agreed to follow up the African successes with an offensive against Sicily, to knock Italy out of the war. This delay in establishing a second front resulted in a severely strained alliance with Russia. The Russians felt, with justification, that they had been thrown to the wolves.

At the Washington Conference in May 1943 Roosevelt and Churchill agreed on a cross-channel invasion set for the spring of 1944 and on a memorandum which defined the primary features of the Allied strategy. Its main points were:

(1) Armament production was to be put into full swing and security of the main areas of war industry were to be given adequate protection.

(2) Essential communications were to be maintained.

(3) The ring around Germany was to be tightened.

(4) German resistance was to be undermined and destroyed by strategic bombing, naval blockade, subversive activities and propaganda.

(5) The development of combined offensive action against Germany was to be continued.

(6) Positions in the Pacific which would safeguard vital interests and deny the Japanese access to raw materials important to her continuous war efforts were to be maintained while at the same time concentrating on the ultimate defeat of Germany. This memorandum practically quoted the British draft brought to Washington. The Americans were uneasy about it but only made slight modifications.

The first aircraft of the US Army Air Force to arrive in the Middle East Theater were 23 B-24D Liberators, commanded by Colonel Harry A Halverson, on their way to bomb Japan from strategic airfields in China under the operational control of the 14th Air Force. The seriousness of the Middle East situation led to Halverson's aircraft being diverted to Egypt. From there they were to attack the oil refineries at Ploesti, in Romania, which were the greatest single sources of fuel for the Nazi war effort.

On 11 June 1942, between 2235 and 2300 hours, Halverson took off from Fayid, Egypt, with 13 B-24Ds and proceeded individually toward the Ploesti oil fields. The bombing run was made at dawn, on 12 June. One attacked the port of Constantia, ten bombed the Astra Romana Refinery and two hit unidentified targets. Opposition to the raid was slight but the extreme distance took its toll. Nine aircraft made it back to Allied territory, one crashed on landing and four were forced to land in Turkey and were interned for the duration of the war. The damage assessment had been very slight. However, the raid raised the hopes and morale of the otherwise demoralized Allies; it proved, like its counterpart raid by Doolittle against Japan, that the war could be taken to the very heart of enemy territory.

This mission also proved, without doubt, the long-range effectiveness of

the B-24, but it also alerted the enemy defense system to the very real danger of possible future strikes from the south. The B-24s of the 98th and 376th Bombardment Groups, which were the first to operate from the Middle East, continued offensive missions against both enemy ground targets in the Western Desert and Axis shipping in the Mediterranean, moving westwards with the Allied advance.

On 23 June 1942 Major General Lewis H Brereton, Commander of the 10th Air Force in India, received orders from General George C Marshall directing him to proceed at once to Fayid, Egypt to assume command of the United States Army Middle East Air Force (USAMEAF). On 28 June 1942 Brereton arrived with a staff of Brigadier General Elmer E Adler, Colonel Victor H Straher and Major Courtney Whitney, 165 enlisted men and seven B-17Es to achieve the mission.

Brereton's B-17Es together with Halverson's B-24s applied constant pressure to enemy forces from 2–9 July with excellent results for so small a force. A total of 21 attacks had been made during July against such targets as Navarino Bay, Greece, Suda Bay,

Above: *Douglas C-47 transport over the Pyramids in Egypt.*
Below: *Chow time at a camp near Bizerta, Tunisia in November 1943.*

Crete, Tobruk and enemy convoys in the Mediterranean. These strikes did a great deal of damage to Axis supply lines despite the small number of USAAF bombers. On 19 July the strength of USAMEAF was nineteen B-24s and nine B-17Es, of which, only ten were operational. After 36 days of operation eleven aircraft were lost. While the force continued to attack German supply routes, convoys, communications and positions, two new bombardment groups and one fighter group was on the way. The 12th Bombardment Group (M), 98th Bombardment Group (H) and the 57th Fighter Group began arriving between 17–30 July.

All of the new groups entered combat by the end of August. This was the exact time that Rommel decided to resume the offensive and break through to Alexandria. He was to discover, in the following hectic four days of intense and bloody fighting that his day as the Desert Fox had passed. On 30 August reconnaissance aircraft observed heavy enemy concentrations on the southern sector of El Alamein. By 2330hrs, a fully fledged offensive had been initiated. Attack and counterattack continued until the 4 September when the battle lines restabilized.

During the six-day offensive, 652 light bombardment sorties were initiated against enemy positions, including 47 sorties of B-25s of the 12th Group. The 3 September saw the largest full-scale air operation conducted of the battle when 18 B-25s, 90 Bostons and 92 Baltimore sorties were flown, escorted by 21 Tomahawk, 60 P-40Fs and 156 Kittyhawks.

The stunning performance of the USAAF groups, especially the 12th Bombardment Group and the 57th Fighter Group (the latter flew 150 sorties in the last four days of the battle), earned the admiration and respect of Air Vice-Marshal Coningham.

The end of September saw the scope of USAAF action in the desert mounting to quite considerable figures. The 12th Bombardment Group had carried out 121 missions, 144 sorties and dropped 139 tons of bombs during 455 flying hours, with a loss of six aircraft. The 57th Fighter Group had flown 46 missions, 290 sorties with only one aircraft shot down.

The winter of 1942–43 was the turning point of the war. The first step in the Allies advance was in North Africa. One of the battles began on 8 November 1942 and was called Operation Torch. Three Anglo-American amphibious landings under the command of General Dwight D Eisenhower were successfully made at Casablanca, Oran and Algiers. Negotiations with Vichyite administrators of these invaded French territories led to the decision to work with the Vichy regime rather than installing a De Gaullist and this decision proved justified. Just before the landings in North Africa the Axis had a grave reverse in Egypt, where the British under General Bernard Montgomery initiated an all-out offensive against the German commander, Field Marshal Erwin Rommel, 'The Desert Fox'. Montgomery broke the Axis line and pursued Rommel across Libya to Tripoli.

Meanwhile, the major emphasis from September–October was on training for the forthcoming British offensive at El Alamein. The only sorties flown during this period were against enemy airfields. Finally, all was in readiness for the coming attack. But General Montgomery would not initiate any attack until air superiority had been gained by the Allied Air Forces. On 19 October the strategic air offensive began to:

(a) elimate any enemy air opposition;

(b) destroy communications and supply facilities in the Tobruk Sector;

(c) undermine the morale of the German troops.

A total of 409 Allied sorties were flown against enemy airfields in 72 hours. The 22 and 23 October saw intense strikes flown against major enemy fields as far out as Maleme Field on Crete. Montgomery now had complete air cuperiority. On 23 October at 2140 hours, the entire El Alamein line erupted into flame with one of the most ferocious artillery barrages of the war. The Battle of El Alamein was now in full gear. The Allies had the following air superiority: fighters, two to one; light bombers, 3.5 to one; and heavies, 2.5 to 0.5.

Above: *Eisenhower celebrates the conquest of Tunis with Giraud in May 1943.*

The entire efforts of the USAMEAF was in support of ground forces along the El Alamein line. The Luftwaffe made a gallant effort to counter Allied air superiority on 26 October to no avail. The Luftwaffe lost six ME 109s, eight MC 202s and three JU 87s, with a further twelve probably destroyed. This was the end of the Luftwaffe in North Africa.

On 27 October the British expanded their salient into the northern German lines. While P-40s of the 64th and 65th Fighter Squadrons jumped twenty CR 42s, escorted by 40 ME 109s and Stukas, the P-40s destroyed seven, with six probables for no losses. This period of intense fighting saw the 12th Group fly over 300 sorties, and the 57th Group 743 sorties completely outclassing the Luftwaffe. The 57th claimed six probables, fifteen damaged and 27 destroyed. USAMEAF losses were one heavy bomber, two medium bombers and two fighters. During the entire battle of El Alamein and its aftermath, Allied air superiority was proven again and again to the total discomfort of Rommel. The USAMEAF was redesignated US 9th Air Force, 12 November 1942 and was to become one of the greatest tactical air forces of all times.

Montgomery's January attack on Tripoli was to end Italy's Empire in North Africa.

Ninth Bomber Command moved to the Gambut area to have closer access to the forward section. With all heavy units moving to Gambut, a section of the 12th Bombardment Group flew to Algiers in late February to assist air units attacking the west. The 81st and 82nd Squadrons were detached on loan to 12th Air Force.

Their first mission was to attack the Holy Moslem City of Tunisia, Kairouan, with P-38s as fighter cover. For reasons never discovered, the P-38s left before schedule, leaving the B-25s to continue alone. The target was to hit as planned but on the return run, the B-25 force was jumped by ME 109s. Only one B-25 was destroyed and the gunners were credited with seven probables.

Rommel had meanwhile retreated to the temporary safety of the Mareth Line in Tunisia, but finally, in mid-February, he attacked the US Second Corps through the Kasserine Pass, making large gains. In fact, the Allied situation had been severe; all air units had been grounded due to extremely bad weather. But now unhindered, they were able to strike enemy targets nonstop. The B-25s of the 12th Group hit railway yards at Gafsa, a bridge near the Kasserine Pass and flew troop harassment raids. Finally, the German advance was halted on 23 February.

The remaining battle for North Africa continually went against the Germans until finally on 8 March, Rommel was recalled to Germany. The German North African armies now came under the command of Colonel General Jurgen von Arnim.

The Axis forces were firmly bottled up in Tunisia by April, with the Cape Bon peninsula at their rear. These troop concentrations were constantly battered by the Western Desert Air Forces, 12th USAF, 9th USAF and 6th Bomber Wing of the RAF, from Bizerta to Tunis. German and Italian air transports brought in supplies from the Naples area and Sicily to the beleaguered troops. But their movements were recorded by photo reconnaissance and radar and the Allied Air Forces were waiting for the right opportunity to pounce on them.

The first telling strike was by P-38s of the 12th AF who destroyed eleven JU 52 transports and five escorts on 5 April. This pressure continued right up to 13 May when all Axis forces in Tunisia surrendered. Thus ended the war in North Africa.

The next operation was Corkscrew, the conquest of Pantelleria, an Italian island, 60 miles from the western coast

Above: *Members of the first all-black Fighter Squadron.*

Below: *The famous French Spahis, during a presentation of P-40s.*

Above: *B-25 bears the triumphant slogan 'Finito Benito, Next Hirohito' over the Gulf of Naples.*

North American B-25J Mitchell

Fuselage: 67ft 7in
Length: 52ft 11in
Height: 15ft 9in
Wing area: 610sq ft
Fuel capacity: 811 imperial gallons
Max range: 1275 miles
Max speed: 275mph at 15,000ft
Initial climb: 1110ft/min
Armament: 13 ×0.5in Brownings

of Sicily and which commanded the Sicilian straits. It was needed by the Allies as an additional fighter base for direct support of Operation Husky. Corkscrew was an attempt to conquer Pantelleria, Lampedusa, and Linosa.

The island itself was extremely rocky and was honeycombed with tunnels and its nickname 'the Gibraltar of the Central Mediterranean' was well-established. It was thought to be impregnable. The amphibious assault never came though; twenty nonstop days and nights of extremely heavy air bombardment proved too much for the 11,199-man garrison who surrendered without even a skirmish. Pantelleria was the first military area to surrender from air attacks alone.

The capture of the other islands of the Pelagie group followed soon after. The airfields were rapidly made serviceable for operation for the P-40. Twenty days later, US engineers successfully completed another airstrip on tiny Gozo, an island fairly close to Malta.

The night of 9–10 July 1943 was D-Day for Husky; the Allied forces were ready to launch their assault against the southern exposed 'underbelly' of Europe. Sicily was not going to be a pushover; it had dealt a history of setbacks to the Greeks, Carthaginians, Romans, and Normans. It was mountainous with precipitous gorges and ravines, winding roads – an island made ready for defense by Mother Nature. It was a natural fortress.

Once the beach landings were completed and the Allied forces moved into the country, there was little to fear from the Luftwaffe. For 45 days prior to D-Day, Allied air units had pounded targets in Sicily, Italy and Sardinia. The air attacks increased in the few

Below: *Airborne infantrymen prepare for take-off from a Sicilian base.*

days directly preceding the invasion, knocking out airfields at Catania, Gerbini, Palermo.

Air superiority was maintained throughout the entire operation. By 20 July all key points had been taken in the center of Sicily. Two days later, the north coast was reached by US forces and Palermo fell. On 23 July, the west coast was reached and Trapani fell. The Axis forces were now hemmed in the Messina Peninsula, northeast Sicily. By 24 July it was the only haven left and the Allies were pushing hard.

Sicily saw the end of the Regia Aeronautica, and it broke the Luftwaffe's power in the central Mediterranean; the Allies lost 370 aircraft compared to the Axis losses of 200 to 1500 planes not to mention the numerous airfields destroyed and overrun.

Sicily was definitely an Allied victory. But the clear, stark reality was that 60,000 German troops had faced 467,000 Allied troops in battle for 38 days – instead of the planned fourteen days. Insofar as the Allies had air and naval superiority, the Germans managed to withstand Italy's defection and evacuate their troops to the mainland – a triumph in itself.

The one direct result of the Sicilian victory was the formal surrender of Italy. Marshal Badoglio signed the armistice on 3 September 1943, the actual day the British 8th Army crossed the Messina Straits. Italy was out of the war.

Allied planning for a landing in Italy was initiated immediately after the Algiers discussion between Churchill, Marshall and Eisenhower. As the pace quickened, additional planning responsibility, unable to be undertaken in Washington and London, was forced upon the field commander. In this instance Eisenhower's task was not easy. The decision made at the Trident Conference the week before, gave Eisenhower freedom to choose an objective but took away much of his striking power. The campaign in Italy was a strategic holding attack. It was to divert German strength to a theater far from the Normandy beaches.

In the fall of 1943, a number of strategies were open to the Allies. The

Above: *Members of the 837th Engineer Aviation Battalion attend class at a US air base in Italy.*

Below: *Stone hut built by GIs at a Liberator base in southern Italy.*

Above: *Ruins of the monastery of Monte Cassino.*
Left: *An ammunition dump goes up 26 seconds after bombs are dropped from a B-26 formation over La Spezia.*

removal of Italy from the war would result in the loss of over 60 divisions to the Axis. Thirty-two of these were stationed in the Balkans and seven in southern France. Hitler would have to replace these immediately, especially those in the Balkans. The possibility of an Allied invasion of the Balkans weighed heavily on Hitler's mind. It was from there he drew vital supplies for his war industry and where Allied forces could join the Russian advance.

By a process of elimination, an assault on the Italian mainland seemed the only course of action, to insure knocking Italy out of the war. As for holding down German divisions, the opinion was that, apart from securing the Alpine frontier, Hitler would deny the Allies the use of the Italian airfields indefinitely and would utilize strong forces to hold the Allies away from northern industrial Italy. The advance into Italy seemed the best strategy to serve the dual requirements of removing Italy from the war and tying down a large number of German divisions. Having made the decision, Eisenhower's planners had to face up to the very real problems of a southern invasion of the Italian peninsula. Eisenhower had the advantage on two counts, command of the air and sea.

It was decided that air cover would once again be the key to the situation just as it had in Sicily. As there was no hope of acquiring naval air support, planning had to be based on the operational range of USAAF fighters. Naples and Taranto were just beyond the effective range of fighter cover. In southern Italy to the south of Belve-

dere there were five enemy fighter fields, the most important at Reggio and Crotone. The prior capture of these would allow seaborne assaults north of Naples but also allow time for the Germans to reinforce the area. The site chosen for the assault was the Gulf of Salerno. The enemy fighter airfields at Monte Corvino, only three miles inland, would take up to four fighter squadrons when captured. This was very important as the Germans had close to 600 fighters and 50 night fighters deployed to airfields around Naples and Foggia. The disadvantage of chosing Salerno lay in the fact that it was situated on a coastal plain which was surrounded by mountains which in turn gave the Germans exceptional observation powers and strategic positions above the plain. However, the landing at Salerno was the closest to Naples and the furthest north that could have air support.

Above: *A B-25 Mitchell bomber leaves Monte Cassino after another devastating air raid.*
Right: *Airborne infantryman prior to take-off from a Sicilian air base.*

Before the operations in Sicily were completed the USAAF's were turning their attention to the railway system and to airfield attacks in Italy. The intention of this strategic bombing program was to eliminate the threat of the Luftwaffe and isolate German forces in southern Italy. Major strikes had already been made at Rome and Naples, the Foggia marshaling yards, other yards and railway junctions as far north as Pisa. This meant that B-17s, B-24s and B-26 squadron, their fighter escorts and ground crews were involved in constant operation. From 18 August–2 September bombers had flown 4500 sorties and dropped 6500 tons of bombs on communications.

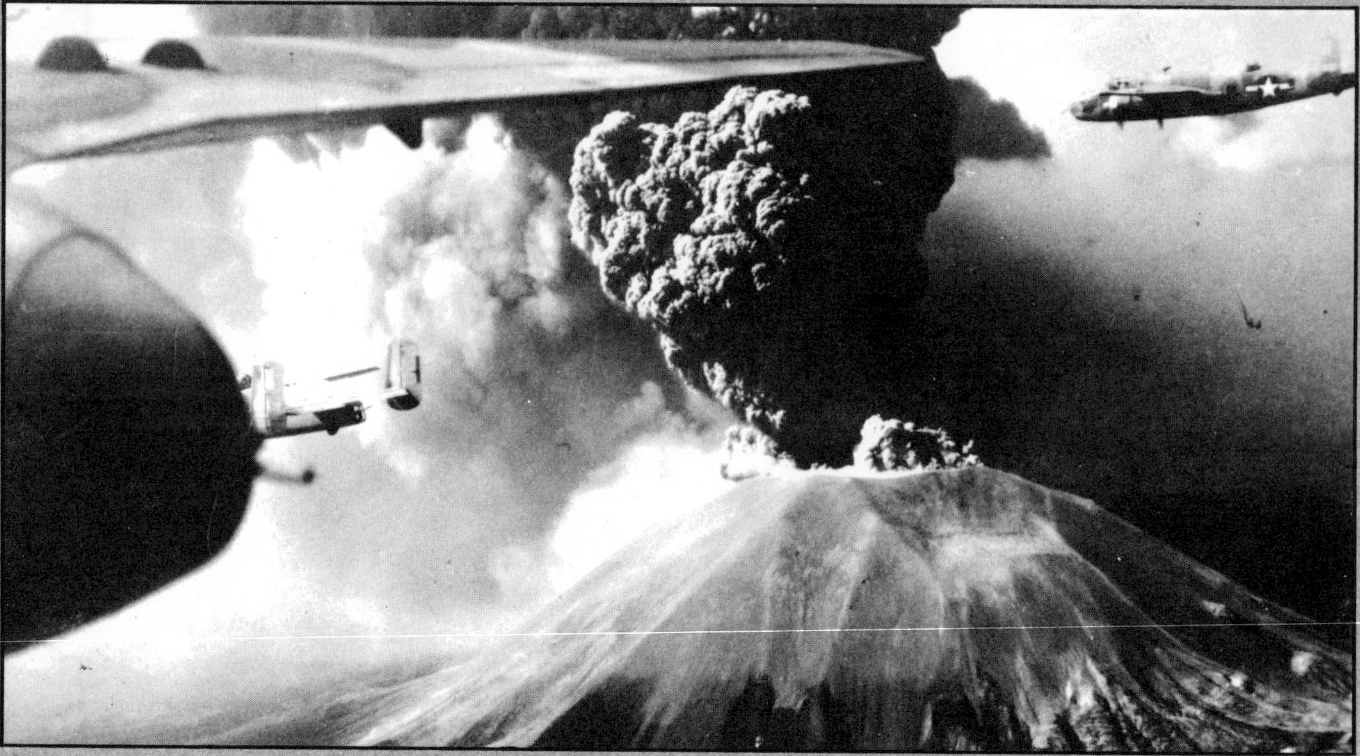

15th Air Force aces (Ten or more kills)

Names	*Victories*	*Groups*
Capt John J Voll	21	31st
Maj Hershel H Green	18	325th
Capt James S Varnell	17	52nd
Maj Samuel J Brown	15	31st
Maj Robert C Curtis	14	52nd
Capt James L Brooks	13	31st
Capt Harry A Parker	13	325th
Maj Michael Brezas	12	14th
Capt Norman C Skogstad	12	31st
Capt Robert J Goebel	11	31st
Lt John B Lawler	11	52nd
Maj William L Leverette	11	14th
Lt Wayne L Lowry	11	325th
Col Charles M McCorkle	11	31st
Maj Norman L McDonald	11	325th
Maj Leland P Molland	11	31st
Capt Robert E Riddle	11	31st
Capt Walter J Goehausen Jr	10	31st

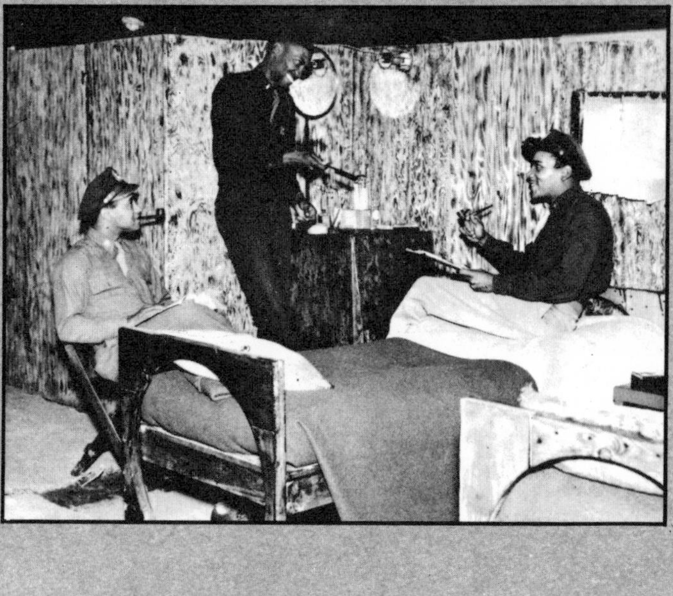

Below: *B-17 of the 15th Air Force drops fire bombs on German positions on the Gothic Line.*
Center left: *B-25s head towards Monte Cassino as they pass over Mount Vesuvius near Naples.*

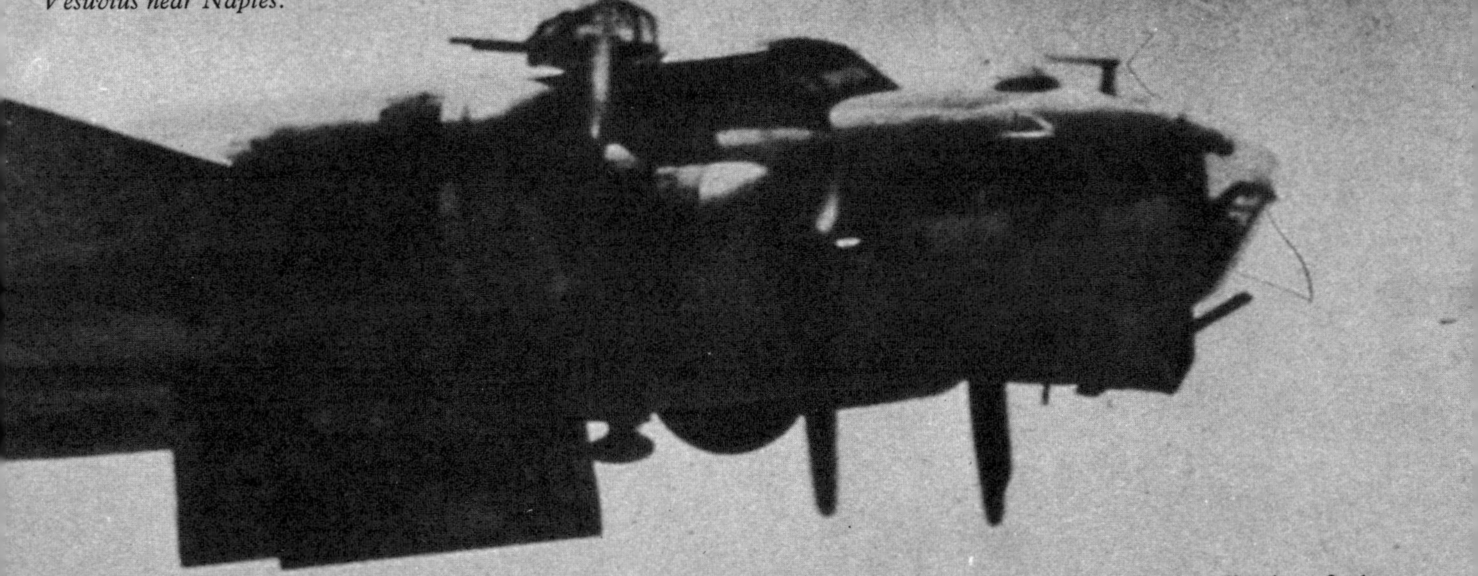

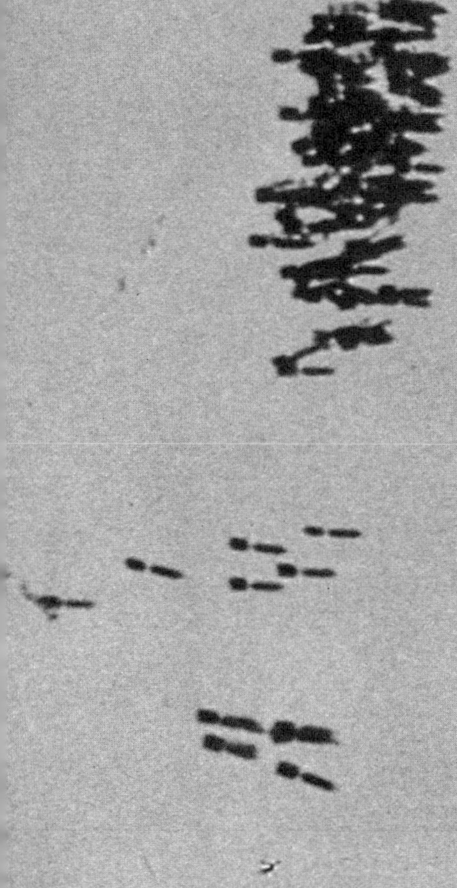

Rail communications and marshaling yards throughout the peninsula were extensively damaged, especially the rails south of Naples-Foggia. The single Luftwaffe attack had been a raid on Bizerta on 17 August by about 100 JU 88s, damaging three ships, sinking an LCI, and causing 240 casualties. Among these was Lt General Horrocks, 10th Corps Commander who was seriously wounded and was relieved by Lt General McCreery. Although the German bomber units were pushed back into central and northern Italy, the fighter squadrons at the Foggia complex were still active. This threat was eliminated on 25 August by a strike of 276 P-38s, which dropped 246 tons of 500lbs general purpose and 20lb fragmentary bombs in 30 minutes on four airfields. The result was 47 Luftwaffe aircraft destroyed and a further thirteen damaged. After this attack there was a noted decline in the Allied bombers lost to German fighters. Previously, as many as 40 German fighters had attacked bomber formations. By September the Luftwaffe was down to less than 600 aircraft in Corsica, Italy, Sardinia and southern France. One-third of these were of low serviceability and the Luftwaffe was only able to fly about 75 sorties a day in the entire area. Meanwhile air operations in support of Avalanche were intensified. On 2 September the systematic bombardment of marshaling yards began, while the light bombers attacked troop concentrations, gun employments and headquarters. Bridges, roads and rail bottlenecks were also hit.

Left: *Black airmen enjoy a respite from bombing missions during the Italian campaign.*
Right: *B-25 unloads its bombs over Monte Cassino.*
Far right: *P-51 Mustang pilot of the Negro Fighter Group is congratulated by its commander, Capt Andrew D Turner. The pilot, Lt Clarence ('Lucky') Lester shot down three Nazi planes on one mission.*

Above: *B-26 of the 12th AF is hit by 88mm shells over Toulon, France.*

The possibility of basing heavies in southern Italy had entered into USAAF planning, and once occupied, a Mediterranean based bomber force was very much in the cards. Italy appeared to have more favorable conditions than Great Britain during the critical winter months. Southern Italy brought into range targets in southern Germany and eastern Europe beyond the operational capabilities of the 8th Air Force. For instance, the Regensburg and Wiener Neustadt factories were more accessible. The Ploesti oil fields were also within easy reach of Italian airfields. General Arnold weighed the existing factors and ordered the creation of the 15th Air Force in the Mediterranean Theater of

Above left: *Monte Cassino*
Left: *B-24 Liberator taking off for a mission in the Po Valley.*

Above: *B-24 Liberator after being hit by shells which crumpled its wing. It crashed but two men bailed out.*
Below: *P-38 Lightnings in formation over Yugoslavia.*

Operations (MTO). This was against the desires of his commanders, especially Ira C Eaker, who felt his 8th Air Force would again lose valuable men and aircraft.

There were definite disadvantages in establishing another numbered air force in Italy:

(1) It was not known for sure if the weather advantage was real or not.

(2) The base facilities in the Foggia area were atrocious.

(3) The Alps created a very real hazard.

Against the disadvantages the 15th Air Force was officially created on 1 November 1943. It had four B-17 and two B-24 groups assigned. These groups had previously been assigned to the 12th AF, but the 12th AF now became the US tactical air force for the MTO. Of course, six bombardment groups would not be enough for the programmed mission of the 15th AF. This was provided by diverting fifteen groups from the 8th AF, just as Eaker had feared. The final group total was 41 groups for the 8th and 21 for the 15th AF.

Principal USAF aircraft utilized during the Italian campaign

Bombers	*Maximum Speed*	*Service Ceiling*	*Range*	*Bomb Load*	*Armament*
B-17 Fortress	295 at 25,000ft	35,000ft	1100	6000lbs	13 × 0.5in or 12.7mm
B-24 Liberator	270 at 20,000ft	27,000ft	2290	4000lbs	10 × 0.5in
A-20 Boston	320 at 11,000ft	24,500ft	1570	2000lbs	5 × 0.5in
A-30 Baltimore	302 at 11,000ft	22,000ft	950	2000lbs	10 × 0.3in 4 × 0.303in
B-25 Mitchell	292 at 15,000ft	20,000ft	1635	4000lbs	6 × 0.5in
B-26 Marauder	305 at 15,000ft	28,000ft	1200	4000lbs	11 × 0.5in
Fighters					
P-39 Airacobra	385 at 11,000ft	35,000ft	675	1 ×500lbs	1 × 37mm 4 × 0.5in
P-40 Warhawk	364 at 20,000ft	35,000ft	610	1600lbs	6 × 0.5in
P-47 Thunderbolt	420 at 26,000ft	35,000ft	590	2 ×1000lbs	8 × 0.5in
P-38 Lightning	414 at 25,000ft	35,000ft	460	1600lbs	1 × 20mm 4 × 0.5in

The Messerschmitt factories at Wiener Neustadt became the 15th AF's first mission, on 2 November 1943. One hundred and twelve B-17s and B-24s were dispatched and the result was that the heaviest damage of the war to date was sustained at Wiener Neustadt. The 15th AF lost eleven bombers. Following this exceptional mission, the 15th AF flew against strategic targets in northern Italy, southern France and the Balkans.

At this time, Arnold thought it was time to initiate a few changes in his air force commanders in Europe. Lt General Ira C Eaker transferred from the 8th to take command of the Mediterranean Allied Air Force (MAAF). Major General Doolittle left the 15th and assumed command of the 8th, Major General Walter F Twig moved from the Pacific Theater and assumed command of the 15th, and General Carl A Spaatz returned to England and assumed command of the US Strategic Air Forces in Europe (USSTAF), HQ at Bushy Park, London. The USSTAF commander had overall authority for all USAAF activities in Europe.

In January 1944 the first six B-24 groups to reinforce the 15th arrived from the US. The B-24 Liberator would be the primary weapon of the 15th AF, just as the Fortress was of the 8th. On 20 February, the 15th was committed to the support of the first

Left: *Martin B-26 Marauder over St Tropez, France during a mission by the 12th AF in August 1944 during Operation Anvil.*
Below: *Bombers of the 9th AF pass over the Alps.*
Below right: *Waves of B-24 Liberators fly into the target area, the Concordia Vega oil refinery, Ploesti, Rumania, 31 May 1944.*

9th Air Force aces (ten or more kills)

Name	*Group*	*Victories*
Capt Don M Beerbower	354 FG	15.5
Lt Col Jack T Bradley	354 FG	15
Capt Lowell K Brueland	354 FG	12.5
Capt Bruce W Carr	354 FG	14
Capt Kenneth H Dahlberg	354 FG	14
Lt Col Glenn T Eagleston	354 FG	18.5
Maj Clyde B East	10 PRG	12
Maj Wallace N Emmer	354 FG	14
Lt Carl M Frantz	354 FG	11
Lt Col James H Holland	354 FG	12.3
Capt Frank Q O'Connor	354 FG	10.75
Lt Col Robert W Stephens	354 FG	13
Lt Col Richard E Turner	354 FG	11

12th Air Force aces (seven or more kills)

Name	*Group*	*Victories*
Lt William J Sloan	82nd	12
Maj Levi R Chase	33rd	10
F/O Frank D Hurlbut	82nd	9
Lt Sylvan Feld	52nd	9
Lt Louis E Curdes	82nd	8
Col William W Momyer	33rd	8
Lt Col Frank A Hill	31st	7
Lt Claude R Kinsey	82nd	7
Lt Ward A Kuentzel	82nd	7
Maj William L Leverette	14th	7*
Capt Norman L McDonald	52nd	7
Maj Herbert E Ross	14th	7
Maj Harley C Vaughn	82nd	7
Lt Edward T Waters	82nd	7

* Later 4 additional victories with 15th Air Force

Anzio beachhead. This meant that it did not participate in the first 1000 bomber raids. Regensburg was attacked by the 8th and 15th AFs on the 25 February. Bombing results were good but the cost was high – 226 bombers lost. The 15th had dispatched 176 B-17s and 20 percent were lost, a substantial loss.

In April the 15th AF struck at Ploesti and had good results. All through the summer and fall of 1944, the 15th AF bombers were continuously active. During this period, it managed to do slightly better than the 8th AF on bombing accuracy. But although leading on bombing accuracy, its loss ratio was much higher than the 8th's. This was probably due to rougher terrain and a lack of coordinated escort procedures.

By August, with a loss of 350 bombers, the 15th AF had practically eliminated the Ploesti oil refineries. Now it turned its attention to the synthetic plants in the eastern and southern sections of Germany. These industrial complexes were cleverly constructed to facilitate fast repairs. Therefore, neutralization required constant bombing by the 15th AF. In only two months, production was cut by 50 percent and with the destruction of Ploesti, by September, it was down a further 25 percent in production.

The 15th AF continued its bombing attack on oil refineries, and produced some of the most accurate strikes of the war, completely destroying some plants. Despite heavy winter clouds, the primary objectives for the strategic bombers in 1945, were communications and oil. Pathfinder methods were used for over 80 percent of the missions flown, and the 15th AF was twice as accurate as the 8th AF, generally attributed to the fact that the 15th had better radar training than the 8th.

Finally, as the strategic targets became few and far between, the 15th AF flew its one and only attack on Berlin, on 24 March 1945. It attacked Prague on 25 March. The remainder of the 15th AF missions were tactical in nature. By 16 April 1945 Spaatz had notified Doolittle and Twig that the strategic air offensive was over.

Below: *Japanese aircraft hit Pearl Harbor, 7 December 1941. A torpedo has hit USS* West Virginia *(center). The USS* Curtiss, Detroit, Raleigh, Utah *and* Tangier *can be seen near Ford Island in this photograph taken at 0800 hrs soon after the first attacks began.*

Pearl Harbor to Midway

In certain respects the US attitude toward World War II did not really differ from the Russians. At the beginning, both countries wanted to stay out of the conflict. As the threat grew, the United States took steps to secure strong outposts which an enemy would have to attack before the country itself. US public opinion turned toward Western Europe between 1939–41, and few appreciated the equally important events which were unfolding in the Pacific. It was realized that Japan was under the control of the militarists who wanted to organize the entire Far East under their radical leadership, in the same way as Hitler planned to dominate Europe. Nevertheless, it was believed that the vast extent of China was a much larger area than Japan could ever hope to conquer and successfully absorb, and the Anglo-American-Dutch navies were a combined force no Japanese government would challenge.

What was not understood was that in the 1930s the Japanese had been building a navy which by 1941 was more powerful than the combined Anglo-American-Dutch forces in the Pacific. The Japanese army and air forces were also of excellent quality. The defeat of France in the spring of 1940 offered Japan an opportunity to occupy northern Indo-China, and in less than a year it seized the entire colony. This gave Japan airfields within striking distance of Singapore and an ever important supply of rice for her people. Meanwhile, Japan's adherence to the Tripartite Pact of September 1940, and its signing of a non-aggression treaty with Russia in April 1941, insured that it would receive little interference from the dominant European powers.

The summer of 1941 saw the crisis in the Pacific reach a peak. The time was ripe to strike. Japan hoped that the United States would remain a source of essential raw materials but in 1938 and 1940, the US had placed trade restrictions on raw materials and manufactured goods exported to Japan. Even so in 1940–41 Japan was still getting four-fifths of her oil and scrap iron from the United States. When the Japanese seized French Indo-China in July 1941, President Roosevelt immediately froze all Japanese assets in the United States. The British and Dutch followed suit. The issue was set: Japan had to stop its aggression and it would be allowed to purchase materials for peacetime needs, or it could take areas which had raw materials and challenge Britain, the United States and the Netherlands to war.

The War Department was not as idle as some people believed; on 26 July 1941, it established a new Far East command and appointed Douglas MacArthur, Commanding General, United States Army Forces in the Far East (USAFFE) and called the Philippine Commonwealth armed forces into the service of the United States. In recalling General MacArthur to active duty, the War Department brought back to the service of the United States one of the most outstanding military figures of American history. His task was truly impossible – to defend the Philippines against the expected Japanese aggression. He immediately placed orders for reinforcements.

Airfields in Hawaii in 1941

Haleiwa	Bellows
Wheeler	Luke
Ewa	Kualoa
Hickam	Barbers Point
Kaneohe	

Above: *A Nakajima B5N Kate torpedo plane takes off from a Japanese carrier on its way to Pearl Harbor as the ship's crew shouts 'Banzai'.*
Left: *Douglas A-20s on maneuvers in North Carolina in November 1941. The US Air Force was painfully unready for a two-front war.*

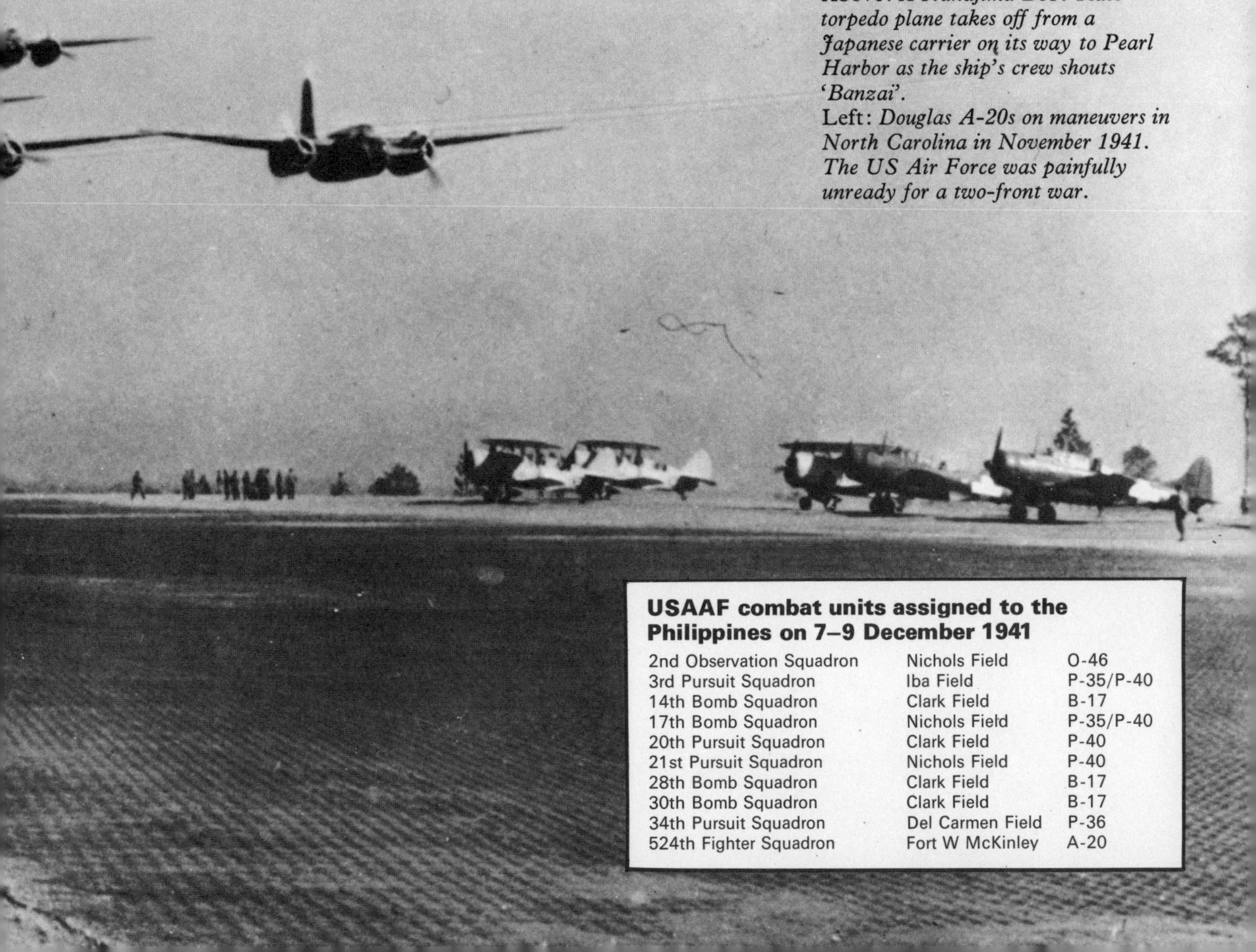

USAAF combat units assigned to the Philippines on 7–9 December 1941

2nd Observation Squadron	Nichols Field	O-46
3rd Pursuit Squadron	Iba Field	P-35/P-40
14th Bomb Squadron	Clark Field	B-17
17th Bomb Squadron	Nichols Field	P-35/P-40
20th Pursuit Squadron	Clark Field	P-40
21st Pursuit Squadron	Nichols Field	P-40
28th Bomb Squadron	Clark Field	B-17
30th Bomb Squadron	Clark Field	B-17
34th Pursuit Squadron	Del Carmen Field	P-36
524th Fighter Squadron	Fort W McKinley	A-20

13th Air Force

Activated: 13 January 1943, New Caledonia

Station:
New Caledonia, 13 January 1943
Espiritu Santo, 21 January 1943
Guadalcanal, 13 January 1944
Los Negros, 15 June 1944
Hollandia, New Guinea, 13 September 1944
Noemfoor, 23 September 1944
Morotai, 29 October 1944
Leyte, 1 March 1945
Clark Field, Luzon, 1 January 1946

Above: *The tattered Stars and Stripes over Hickam Field at 0755 hrs just after Pearl Harbor began.*
Left: *'From Here to Eternity'. The atmosphere at Pearl Harbor before the surprise attack.*

Endeavors to provide the necessary aircraft for the Philippine Department were indeed impressive. In July 1941 130 fighters and 272 bombers, with 68 reserves were allocated for shipment to the Philippines. The route utilized by the B-17s was from Hawaii to Midway and Wake Island, then to Port Moresby and northward to the Philippines. By December 1941 Major General Lewis H Brereton, the Far East Air Force Commander, had 74 medium and heavy bombers, 175 pursuit aircraft and 58 other aircraft in V Bomber Command, V Interceptor Command and his Service Command. At this stage, Brereton had 76 more aircraft than the Hawaiian Department. Numerically, he had three times as many B-17s and P-40Es as the Hawaiian Department, indicating the emphasis placed on the importance of the Philippines by the War Department and the Chief of Staff, General George C Marshall. In November it was decided to send all new model B-17s in the United States to the Philippines, and allocate all B-24s to the Far East Air Force. In fact, the air staff were contemplating sending the remaining twelve B-17s of the Hawaiian Department to the Philippines. The Philippines priority was so high as to totally disrupt the training schedule of the Hawaiian Air Force and to make the air defense of Oahu secondary.

So, far from lacking in quantity and quality, Brereton had the finest aircraft of any US overseas department. The problem was their adequate dispersal – which was to prove fatal and result in the eventual destruction of the Far East Air Force (FEAF) on the ground. If it could have been dispersed and remained intact, the Japanese landings on Luzon might have been prevented and the war in the Pacific taken a different perspective. MacArthur's argument that Roosevelt was not supporting him sufficiently does not hold water in the light of the aforementioned facts.

The idea of a pre-emptive strike against the United States Pacific Fleet at Pearl Harbor developed in the mind

Below: *The remains of a plane destroyed by the Pearl Harbor attack.*

USAAF units/combat assigned to Hawaii on 7–8 December 1941

6th Fighter Squadron	Wheeler Field	P-40
19th Fighter Squadron	Wheeler Field	P-40
19th Troop Carrier Squadron	Hickam Field	C-33
23rd Bomb Squadron	Hickam Field	B-17
26th Bomb Squadron	Hickam Field	B-17
31st Bomb Squadron	Hickam Field	B-17
42nd Bomb Squadron	Hickam Field	B-17
43rd Reconnaissance Squadron	Bellows Field	O-47/B-18
44th Fighter Squadron	Bellows Field	P-40
45th Fighter Squadron	Wheeler Field	P-36
46th Fighter Squadron	Wheeler Field	P-36
47th Fighter Squadron	Wheeler Field	P-36/P-40
72nd Bomb Squadron	Bellows Field	B-17
72nd Fighter Squadron	Wheeler Field	P-40
73rd Fighter Squadron	Wheeler Field	P-40
78th Fighter Squadron	Wheeler Field	P-40
427th Bomb Squadron	Hickam Field	B-17
431st Bomb Squadron	Hickam Field	B-17
531st Fighter Squadron	Hickam Field	B-18/P-40

of Admiral Isoruku Yamamoto, Commander of the Imperial Japanese Combined Fleet, after very successful fleet exercises during 1940. He decided on a swift, decisive air attack to eliminate the US Pacific Fleet base at Pearl Harbor as well as the land based US Army Air Force units based throughout Oahu.

Yamamoto was given the go-ahead for his plan by the Imperial Japanese Staff after the breakdown in negotiations between the United States and Japan. On 26 November 1941 the Japanese task force sailed from Tankan Bay in the Kurile Islands for Hawaii. By 6 December the 31 ships of Admiral Chuichi Nagumo were starting to approach within striking distance of Pearl. His task force consisted of the aircraft carriers *Akagi* and *Kaga*, light carriers *Soryu* and *Hiryu* and the *Shokaku* and *Zuikaku*, each with 70 planes aboard. The remainder of the force was made up of the battleships *Hiei* and *Kirishima*, the cruisers, *Tone*, *Chikuma* and *Abukuma*, nine destroyers and three submarines.

The weather was unexpectedly calm and there was a light fog present which reduced visibility. At 0600hrs, 7 December 1941, 230 miles north of Honolulu, the first wave of 183 aircraft took off under the command of Commander Mitsuo Fuchida. The attack was a complete surprise. Of the 94 ships in port, only one was under way when the dive-bombers hit Hickam and Wheeler Fields. The first assault wave completed its mission in about one hour and had lost only one dive-bomber, five torpedo planes and three fighters.

At 0854hrs, the second wave of 167 aircraft roared in under Commander Shimazaki. This attack lasted for another hour but now US resistance was more determined. The total Japanese losses were nine fighters, fifteen dive-bombers and five torpedo planes. Fuchida stayed over the target area to photograph the results. Besides the destruction of the Pacific Fleet, all US airfields were in flames, and 50 percent of USAAF strength in Oahu was destroyed. A few US aircraft managed to get into the air but their results were only nominal: two P-40B Tomahawk pilots claimed eight bombers; five P-36 Mohawks claimed two Zeros and two more damaged for the loss of two US pursuit aircraft.

Of 231 USAAF aircraft on Oahu, 97 were destroyed and 88 damaged but reparable. US Navy losses totaled 80, more than 50 percent of the total available. This destruction was blamed on the aircraft being parked on the runways wingtip to wingtip to prevent easy access by possible saboteurs. US casualties for the whole attack included 3077 navy and Marines killed in action, 876 wounded in action; 226 army killed in action and 396 wounded in action, totaling 4575 casualties. Japanese deaths numbered 55 airmen. The elimination of the USAAF and the Pacific Fleet were major objectives of Japan. With the virtual total destruction of the Far East Air Force the same day, in the Philippines, there was practically no airpower remaining in the Pacific Theater.

Several hours after the Pearl Harbor tragedy, at exactly 1240 hours (Philippine time), on 8 December 1941, 54 Japanese aircraft launched their attacks against the US Forces in the Philippines by bombing, strafing and almost completely destroying Clark Field, the large air base in the Plains of Central Luzon, just northeast of Manila. Nine precious hours were wasted after the news of Pearl Harbor, yet the inactivity of the field is a matter of record. Why did MacArthur and Brereton not act? That is a question which in all probability will never be answered. How a brilliant commander and veteran airman like MacArthur and Brereton could have been caught napping at such a critical time was uncharacteristic of both men. Yet it was a mistake which caused the loss of two irreplaceable B-17D squadrons of the 19th Bombardment Group (H) which should have been redeployed to Mindanao 48 hours earlier, and all the P-40s except four which managed to take off and engage the enemy.

The 19th Bomber Group was formed in 1929, and was designated a Heavy Bombardment Group in 1939. It moved to the Philippines from New Mexico in September–November 1941, with B-17 Flying Fortresses. The Group had only become operational 30 days before the actual attack on Clark Field.

The Imperial Japanese Air Force planes flying in two 'V' formations of 27 aircraft each, suddenly appeared over the towering Zambales Mountain Range, northwest of Clark Field. They walked their bombs diagonally across the field beginning with the row of officers quarters and ripping through the parked P-40s and B-17Ds, the present day 13th Air Force HQ and what is now the Base Motor Pool area. The bombs from the second wave followed almost immediately in the same pattern. This stunning surprise attack left Clark Field ablaze.

Ninety percent of the structures and buildings had been hit and many more were on fire. One enemy bomb knocked out the communications center and left the field in complete isolation. The only opposition came from the four P-40s led into the air before the attack by Lt Joseph H Moore (a former 7th Air Force Commander in Vietnam and a Lt General). Engaging one of the incoming Zeros, 2nd Lt Randall Keaton shot one down immediately and later earned the coveted Silver Star for downing the first Japanese aircraft over the Philippines in World War II.

The 93rd Bombardment Squadron (H), however, was on tactical maneuvers at Del Carmen Field and escaped the attack. Ground support and supplies were hastily moved from Clark Field to safe points and aircraft that had not sustained severe damage were dispatched to Del Carmen Field.

To make matters even worse, shortly after 1230 hours, a formation of 54 Japanese bombers and 50 Zeros flying fighter cover, totally surprised the garrison of Iba Field, 40 miles west of Clark Field and virtually annihilated its P-40 squadrons, which had just returned from the South China Sea out of fuel. So by 1500 hours, 8 December 1941, the strength of MacArthur's

Far East Air Force (FEAF) was reduced by 67 percent: only seventeen B-17s on Mindanao remained of the original 35 heavy bombers, and only seventeen of the P-40s were left intact. Also 33 older military aircraft were destroyed. Only seven Japanese aircraft had been destroyed. In relation to Pearl Harbor losses, casualties were moderate: 83 killed and 154 wounded at Clark, Iba and Del Carmen Fields. The overall result of this attack was the elimination of the Far East Air Force as an effective fighting force on Day One of the war.

The remainder of the B-17Ds fought a gallant rearguard action, bombing Japanese shipping routes, and targets from Mindanao, Java and ultimately Australia, until the last survivor, the famous 'Swoose' (40-3097) was ordered back to the United States early in 1942. The overwhelming Japanese destruction of the FEAF was (in my opinion) one of the most single important contributing factors in the loss of the Philippines. With five airfields on Luzon alone, and with his air force intact, MacArthur could have possibly stopped the Japanese invasion of Luzon, 10–24 December 1941, or so severely impeded it, that the whole scope of the war in the western Pacific would have changed.

With the Philippines intact and serving as a base of operations, the Far East Air Force could have wreaked havoc with the Japanese trade and supply routes, transportation and communications network and would have prevented the Japanese from achieving their long-range objectives.

The Pearl Harbor attack resulted in several lengthy investigations and the removal of the top commanders in Hawaii; the Clark fiasco did not even produce a single inquiry. It seems ironic that the most mortal of military blunders, that of being taken by surprise was practically overlooked by the War Department, except for a telephone reprimand for Major General Lewis H Brereton, Commander of the Far East Air Force from General Henry Arnold, received the same day.

For twenty days after the tactical blunder which virtually eliminated the Far East Air Force, Brereton attempted, but to no avail, to revamp and revitalize his decimated air squadrons in order to halt the enemy's air advance across the Philippines. Despite gallant efforts by FEAF fighters, Japanese air formations bombed Nichols Field and Cavite Naval Air Station, south of Manila, on 10 December 1941, with devastating results. The Japanese had conducted fourteen air strikes against strategic locations around Manila by 12 December. The FEAF rose to the challenge each time but all in vain;

Below: *Wrecked B-17 at Bellows Field, Hawaii after a forced landing during the Pearl Harbor assault.*

with its strength decimated, no hope of reinforcements and spare parts unavailable it was a hopeless gesture to say the least. By Christmas Eve 1941, the FEAF was practically nonexistent and MacArthur ordered Brereton to Australia to re-establish FEAF Headquarters, organize advance attack bases and to support the defense of the Philippines by the US Army Air Force in the Far East.

The men in Australia moved to Java by 31 December 1941 and, operating LB-30, B-17 and B-24 aircraft, earned a Distinguished Unit Citation (DUC) for applying constant pressure on enemy transports, aircraft, ground installations and warships during the Japanese drive through the Philippines and the Dutch Indies in early 1942. The 19th Bombardment Group (H) returned to Australia in March 1942, and in late March evacuated General Douglas MacArthur, his family and battle staff from the Philippines. After a short rest this group resumed combat operations, participating in the Battle of the Coral Sea and attacking Japanese transportation, communications and ground forces during the enemy's invasion of Papua.

Meanwhile Brigadier General H H George, commander of the FEAF Interceptor Command that remained in the Philippines, continued to pit his ever-decreasing force of P-35 and P-40 aircraft against the overwhelming strength of the Japanese. The FEAF put up a courageous but ineffectual fight against sheer superior enemy strength and aircraft; from that first eventful day, 8 December 1941, they were doomed. This turn of events

5th Bomber Command

Activated: 14 November 1941

Station:
Clark Field, Luzon, 14 November 1941
Darwin, Australia, December 1941
Java, January–March 1942
Townsville, Australia, 5 September 1942
Port Moresby, New Guinea, December 1942
Nadzab, New Guinea, 21 February 1944
Owi, Schauten Islands, 15 August 1944
Leyte, November 1944
Manila, January 1945
Clark Field, Luzon, March 1945
Okinawa, August 1945
Murayome, Japan, October 1945
Irumagawa, Japan, 15 January–31 May 1946

was to be reversed in October 1944, and the United States Army Air Force was to play a prime role in the reconquest of the Philippines.

The surrender of Bataan and Corregidor marked the end of any real, organized resistance to Japanese conquest of their new territory. In just four months, from Pearl Harbor on 7 December 1941 to the fall of Corregidor on 8 May 1942, the 19th Bombardment Group raided airfields, ground installations and shipping near Rabaul, New Britain, picking up another Distinguished Unit Citation for three very hazardous missions. The Medal of Honor was posthumously awarded to Captain Harold Pease Jr for his herioc action on 6–7 August 1942; when one engine of his bomber failed over New Britain, he returned to Australia to find another operational plane. He selected the best available aircraft and rejoined his outfit for an attack on a Japanese airfield near Rabaul; by exceptional flying he maintained his position in the formation until his bombs were released on the target, in the fight that raged on after the bombers had left the target area, Pease's aircraft sustained battle damage and fell behind the main formation and was lost. Men of Pease's courage were to be found in all theaters and his action epitomized the American fighting man's ideal throughout the war.

After the dual attack on 7 December 1941, on Pearl Harbor and the Philippines, the Japanese turned their attention on the British. On 10 December two British battleships, *Prince of Wales* and *Repulse*, were sunk while off the eastern coast of Malaya by a superb torpedo attack. Next to fall was the impregnable fortress of Singapore, and with its capitulation went the last chance of a unified defense of Southeast Asia.

Below: *Training planes in a line at Randolph Field, Texas. These aircraft were immediately flown to the Pacific after Pearl Harbor.*

In late December the American, British, Dutch and Australian (ABDA) command was established with General Wavell in command. On 24 January 1942, it engaged a Japanese invasion force off Balikpapan, Borneo but could not impede its advance. Three weeks later Bali and Timor were attacked and Darwin was severely damaged by a swift striking carrier force. The 27 February saw the gallant remains of the ABDA fight the hopeless Battle of the Java Sea. The Dutch Admiral Karel Doorman commanded the Allied surface fleet in a running two-day battle against overwhelmingly superior Japanese naval strength. The heavy cruisers *USS Houston, HMS Exeter*, gun cruisers *HNMS De Ruyter* and *Java*, and *HMAS Perth* were all sunk. In 90 days Allied naval strength in Southeast Asia was virtually wiped out. In the Central Pacific US naval power had been effectively neutralized and the Japanese were preparing for their next step, Midway. But the United States was already planning a strike at the very heart of Japan. In April 1942 Colonel James H Doolittle, one of America's foremost aviators, led sixteen modified Mitchell B-25 medium bombers, flown by volunteer crews, from the flight deck of the *USS Hornet*.

The target was Tokyo. It was to be a token raid to raise the spirits of the people back home and the morale of the troops overseas. The *USS Hornet* intended to approach within 400 miles of Japan to allow Doolittle's aircraft adequate range to fly on and refuel near Chungking, China. But the *Hornet* was spotted 800 miles out by a Japanese patrol boat and the launch could no longer be delayed even with the added mileage. All sixteen aircraft took off safely and the attack was a complete surprise. The hard part came next as the aircraft attempted to reach China. They encountered various hardships and were forced to bale out and ditch their planes. Most of the crews made it back to their units, except for eight captured by the Japanese; three were shot. Another crew which landed at Vladivostok was interned.

The raid caused little damage and resulted in four Japanese fighter groups remaining in the home islands to prevent this type of incident from happening again. It also proved that the Japanese could be reached by our air force and morale rocketed. The entire raid was the work of one man, an outstanding individual and superb pilot, Jimmy Doolittle, one of the great proponents of air power.

At the end of May 1942 seven Japanese Imperial Naval aircraft carriers sailed in three separate groups for a coordinated major fleet operation, the primary objective being the capture of Midway Island, 1135 miles WNW of Pearl Harbor and the westernmost outpost of the Hawaiian Islands. Claimed by the United States in 1867, this atoll was situated midway across the Pacific Ocean, placing it in a very strategic location. Its importance as a tactical air base was second only to Pearl Harbor itself. Midway could not be allowed to fall into Japanese hands. Midway also saw the beginning of 'Combined Operations', something which has remained with us until the present time.

Yamamoto, the Imperial Japanese Fleet Admiral, sent the aircraft carriers *Ryujo* and *Junyo* to cover the assault and occupation of Attu and Kiska Islands, in the Aleutians. The *Zuiho* was attached to the central group and could go to the aid of either the Aleutian or Midway task force whichever was required. The main force consisted of Yamamoto's flagship the *Yamato*, two other battleships, a cruiser, the light cruiser *Hosho* and twelve destroyers.

But the principal role was in the hands of Vice Admiral Chuichi Nagumo's First Carrier Striking Force, leading the First Carrier Division, consisting of the *Akagi* and *Kaga*. Rear Admiral Yamaguchi commanded the Second Carrier Division, made up of the *Hiryu* and the *Soryu*. The carriers were to receive their cover from the battleships *Haruna* and *Kirishima*, and the heavy cruisers *Chikuma* and *Tone*, commanded by Rear Admiral Abe. A further eleven destroyers and the cruiser *Nagara* would accompany the carrier force as a screening group.

Nagumo's primary role was to launch a pre-emptive strike against Midway to soften up if possible the USAAF defense units stationed there. The attack was to be launched on 4 June 1942, 24 hours before the actual landings by the Occupation Force. Japanese plans for Midway were known in advance by Admiral Nimitz, due to the US Navy's Combat Intelligence Unit at Pearl Harbor breaking their code in early 1942. By 15 May Nimitz knew positively that Midway would be the objective of a major Japanese amphibious assault and acted accordingly to strengthen the atoll's defenses. Colonel H Sharmon's 6th Marine Defense Battalion was considerably beefed up and the garrison brought to a total of 2138 Marines. Capt Cyril Simard, commander of the land based air force on Midway, had 1491 airmen and over 120 fighters, bombers and reconnaissance aircraft available. This was an increase of 60 aircraft, including eighteen Dauntless dive-bombers, seven Wildcat fighters, six Avenger torpedo planes, four USAAF B-26 Marauders, eighteen B-17 heavy bombers, and 32 PBY Catalina flying boats.

On 4 June the four Japanese aircraft carriers launched 72 attack aircraft and 36 fighters in a typical dawn strike against the island of Midway. Meanwhile, the three US carriers were 250 miles east, and all 28 Midway-based US Marine Corps fighters were airborne.

Radar directed, 21 F2A-3s and seven F4F-3s intercepted the Japanese B5Ns and D3As and shot down four aircraft and damaged six more. Two A6Ms were destroyed ten minutes later but thirteen F2A-3s and three F4F-3s were destroyed and seven severely damaged. The results were not very promising with only five Midway Marine fighters left after the initial attack.

The Japanese Air Force Commander leading the air attack against Midway was Lt Tomonaga whose bomber task force succeeded in destroying the majority of Midway facilities but US casualties were light with only eleven killed. Japanese losses were estimated at one-third of the attacking force. Tomonaga realized that despite the heavy damage inflicted, Midway's air strength was practically untouched. At 0700 hours he radioed Admiral Nagumo with the following message: 'A second strike is required.'

Meanwhile six Avengers and four B-26 Marauders from Midway were attacking the carriers. The Avengers began their bombing run at 0710 hours, taking heavy anti-aircraft fire and the full attention of the defending Zeros. Three of the Avengers were destroyed before launching their torpedoes and only one actually returned to Midway, and it was severely damaged. The Martin B-26 Marauders came in at 200ft and released their torpedoes at 800yds with no damage to the carriers. Again 50 percent of the attacking force was destroyed; only two Marauders made it back to Midway. The unreliability of the US torpedoes was the major factor behind the unsuccessful attacks.

With these attacks against his carrier force by the land based Midway force, Nagumo had no doubts about the need for a second strike at Midway. At 0715 hours, he ordered the second wave of aircraft to stand ready to attack Midway. All torpedo aircraft and dive-bomoers were to be armed with explosive ordnance appropriate for ground targets. Basically, this was a simple task with the dive-bombers, but on the *Akagi* and *Kaga*, it meant taking the Kates down to the main hangar deck

5th Air Force aces (11 or more victories)

Major Richard J Bong	40
Major Thomas B McGuire Jr	38
Colonel Charles H MacDonald	27
Lt Col Gerald R Johns	22
Colonel Neil E Kearby	22
Major Jay T Rubbins	22
Lt Colonel Thomas J Lynch	20
Major George S Welch	16
Major Edward Crazy	15
Major William D Dunken	15
Major Cyril F Homes	15
Capt Robert M DeHaven	14
Capt David B Easthan	12
Capt Kenneth G Leuld	12
Capt James A Watkins	12
Capt Richard L West	12
Capt Francis J Lent	11
Lt Col John S Loisel	11
Capt Cornelius M Smith Jr	11
Lt Kenneth C Sparks	11

so that the torpedoes could be replaced, a time-consuming process, and one thing Nagumo was running out of fast was time. Practically in the middle of rearming, Nagumo received an important message from the *Tone's* seaplane. Her pilot reported sighting ten enemy surface ships 'bearing 10 degrees, distance 240 miles from Midway'. Now 30 minutes late, Nagumo knew, that he was faced with a major problem. At 0745 hours, he ceased the ordnance change-over and ordered his carrier force to stand by to initiate strikes against the US fleet. At 0752 hours his force again was subjected to a US attack which consisted of sixteen Dauntlesses from Midway. The commander of this inexperienced formation decided to utilize the shallow, glide-bombing technique. This made the dive-bombers virtually defenseless against the Japanese Zeros which were flying combat air patrol (CAP). The results were disastrous; eight Dauntlesses were destroyed and a further six severely damaged. The Japanese battle damage was practically non-existent.

Finally, at 0809 hours, Nagumo received the precious information he had been waiting for concerning the composition of the US task force. The *Tone*'s seaplane radioed that the enemy force was five cruisers and five destroyers. Between 0815–0820 hours his carriers again were attacked by a Midway-based force consisting of fifteen B-17s and eleven Vindicators. The USAAF B-17s bombed from 20,000ft and concentrated on the *Hiryu* and *Soryu*, while the Vindicators outnumbered, outgunned, and considerably slower than the Zeros attacked the battleship *Haruna*. The results of this fifth strike again miraculously caused negative damage to the carrier force. Midway losses were two Vindicators shot down; all other aircraft returned to base.

At 0820 hours the message which was to initiate the downfall of the Imperial Navy's western advance in the Pacific was received: the *Tone*'s seaplane pilot reported, that the enemy force had one carrier in sight directly behind the cruiser/destroyer force. Yamaguchi wanted an immediate launch from the *Hiryu* and *Soryu*. But in reality, Nagumo was in no position to launch an immediate strike. If he did, it would be without fighter cover, as the fighters reserves had been used in defending the carrier force. Besides that the *Akagi* and *Kaga* torpedo bombers were still armed with bombs intended for land-based targets on Midway. On top of this, Tomonaga's strike was returning from Midway with damaged aircraft.

By 0750 hours Rear Admiral Raymond A Spruance realized he could not wait any longer before attacking the Japanese carrier fleet. He ordered Lt Commander McCluskey to prepare for an attack on the Japanese Carrier Force. All naval air units were in the air by 0806 hours, but the F-6 Wildcat cover for Lt Commander Eugene Lindsey's 6th Torpedo Squadron, took an incorrect battle station over the *Hornet*'s 8th Torpedo Squadron, commanded by Lt Commander John Waldron. This error in assuming the correct station meant that both the 6th and 8th Torpedo Squadrons attacked without fighter cover.

Rear Admiral Frank J Fletcher, on the much slower *Yorktown*, had withheld his air units due to the unknown location of the two remaining Japanese aircraft carriers. Finally, at 0839 hours, he launched seventeen Dauntlesses of

Below: *SBD Dauntlesses over the Japanese carrier* Mikuma *during the Battle of Midway, 6 June 1942.*

the 3rd Bomber Squadron, commanded by Lt Commander Massey, and six Wildcat F-6s of the 3rd Fighter Squadron, Lt Commander Thatch in command. Fletcher wisely kept a firm aircraft reserve just in case.

Unknown to the air groups of the *Enterprise* and *Hornet*, Nagumo changed course, resulting in the *Hornet*'s dive bombers and fighters searching to the southeast. The fighters had to ditch as they ran out of fuel while 26 dive-bombers returned to the *Hornet* and fourteen to Midway, where three crashed on the final approach. The 8th Torpedo Squadron was flying lower and became separated by cloud cover, so assumed a westerly course. At 0920 hours Lt Commander Waldron sighted the enemy force to the northwest and began his attack, without fighter cover. His forces sustained heavy anti-aircraft fire and Zeros flying combat air patrol over the carriers hit him 3–5 miles out from the target. The results were disastrous to say the least: all fifteen of the 8th Torpedo Squadron were destroyed.

At 0930 hours the 6th Torpedo Squadron attacked, also without fighter cover. Lt Commander Lindsey ordered his squadron to split and hit the *Kaga* from both sides but as they circled, Zeros came in for the kill. The results of this attack were again devastating: ten Devastators, including Lindsey's were destroyed. This attack was concluded at 1005 hours and shortly after Massey's 3rd Torpedo Squadron sighted the enemy fleet. Nagumo, now becoming decidedly worried, postponed all launchings until he retrieved his Midway strike aircraft which were flying combat air patrol. Then he would reorganize his forces, while moving north to preclude further attacks and, when prepared, would launch one massive strike to totally annihilate the US fleet. Therefore, he ordered all aircraft on the flight deck be brought below until Tomonaga's aircraft safely returned. He also ordered the bombers for the second wave to be rearmed with the torpedoes and armor-piercing ordnance.

At 0837 hours Tomonaga's aircraft started coming in, and the Japanese deck crews were hurrying to rearm the strike aircraft yet again. This bit of haste, resulting in carelessness became a tragedy. They stacked the bombs to be moved on the deck, instead of returning them to the munitions magazines as procedure dictated. Nagumo advised Yamamoto of his plans at 0918 hours, and then changed course to 90 degrees ENE. He planned to launch his strike at 1030 hours with a force of 36 dive-bombers and 54 torpedo bombers. At this time, *Akagi* received reports of large groups of US aircraft approaching and since these could not have come from only one aircraft carrier, *Soryu* dispatched a search plane to ascertain the exact US surface fleet strength and location.

The US carriers had already lost 35 torpedo aircraft in three separate attacks without so much as a single hit. But this had brought the Zeros flying combat air patrol to lower altitudes and consequently, the Japanese carriers without radar had no way of observing the high altitude dive-bombers which were fast approaching. Therefore, unopposed by fighter cover, the US strike dropped their bombs directly on the flight decks chock full of aircraft preparing to take off.

Lt Commander McCluskey failing to find Nagumo's carriers at the designated place made a decision which only the on-the-scene commander could make, and elected to search to the northwest. This was one of those critical decisions, the essence of which is unfathomable. At 1005 hours McCluskey discovered the carriers, thanks to the help of a Japanese destroyer which he had followed back to the carrier force. At 1022 hours he began his attack on the *Kaga* while five Dauntlesses from the 6th Bomber Squadron hit the *Akagi*. One bomb hit the *Akagi* amidship, exploding the bombs which the deck crews had so carelessly left stacked in the hangar deck. A second hit aft, turning Nagumo's flagship into a blazing inferno. At 1047 hours the *Akagi* was aban-

Below: *USS* Yorktown *(CV-5) under attack at the Battle of Midway, 6 June 1942.*

doned, Nagumo transferring his flag to the cruiser *Nagara*. The *Kaga* had sustained four hits which also caused uncontrollable fires to rage throughout the ship; she was abandoned in the aftermath. At 1025 hours the *Yorktown*'s dive-bombers attacked the *Soryu* and within twenty minutes, and after three direct hits, she was also a total loss. In under ten minutes 75 percent of Nagumo's carrier task force was destroyed, not so much due to coordination and planning, but to individual initiative and fantastic luck.

During the evacuation of the *Akagi*, Rear Admiral Abe was in tactical command of the Japanese carrier force. He ordered Yamaguchi's carrier which had so far gone unscathed to launch a strike. At this point the Japanese still had no idea where the US fleet was located because the *Soryu*'s plane had radio difficulty. At 1058 hours, Yamaguchi launched eighteen dive-bombers and six fighters from *Hiryu*, commanded by Lt Michio Koboyashi. The *Yorktown*'s luck was now beginning to run out, as Koboyashi's aircraft managed to follow the returning 3rd Bomber Squadron back to the carrier.

At 1120 hours *Yorktown* launched ten Dauntlesses to search northwest, and by 1200 hours, she had twelve F-6 Wildcats in the air for combat air patrol. Refueling was in progress when radar picked up the approaching Japanese flight formation to the southwest; it was stopped immediately and aircraft launched. Wildcats from the *Enterprise* and *Hornet* went to the Yorktown's aid, bringing her fighter cover to 28 aircraft. Eight of the Japanese dive-bombers made it through the fighters and anti-aircraft cover, and registered three hits on the *Yorktown*. The first caused fires below the main deck; the second resulted in the forward fuel tanks and magazines having to be flooded; and the final one knocked out five of her six boilers. The carrier immediately slowed down to six knots, the radar was inoperative and communications were untenable. Fletcher transferred to the cruiser *Astoria*, and the *Yorktown*'s aircraft were moved to the *Enterprise* and *Hornet*.

At 1235 hours the *Soryu*'s search plane reported the presence of three US aircraft carriers; with this information Yamaguchi launched ten dive-bombers and six fighters for a last strike. By 1335 hours, the *Yorktown*'s damage-control parties had accomplished the impossible, the hole in the flight deck was repaired and four of the five boilers relit. She was again refueling fighters, when radar picked up the approaching attack. The Japanese aimed for what they thought to be an undamaged carrier and struck the *Yorktown* a second time. Two hits breached the port fuel tanks and eliminated all power connections. The pumps became inoperable and counter-flooding virtually impossible. Finally, at 1458 hours, the order was given to abandon ship.

At 1530 hours the *Enterprise* launched 24 dive-bombers and were supported by sixteen more from the *Hornet* at 1630 hours. Revenge for the *Yorktown* was forthcoming. Yamaguchi believed two US carriers were out of action and prepared to launch another strike at 1800 hours, hoping for the dusk element of surprise.

He had no way of knowing that, in fact, the *Yorktown* had been attacked twice. At 1700 hours once again without radar, the *Enterprise*'s dive-bombers undetected hit the *Hiryu*. Four hits were registered and the fires raged so severely, that the *Hornet*'s aircraft unsuccessfully attacked *Tone* and *Chikuma*, 30 minutes later.

The result of Midway was four Japanese aircraft carriers and one heavy cruiser lost to one US carrier and one destroyer lost. One thing that the Japanese lost which they would never be able to replace was 100 experienced pilots. The US victory at Midway against overwhelming odds was the turning point in the Pacific Theater.

Below left: *The Stars and Stripes are lowered on Corregidor after its surrender on 6 May 1942.*
Below: *Japanese troops celebrate the defeat of US armed forces on Bataan in April 1942.*

Over the Jungle

Above: *B-24 Liberator over Makin Island, a new US base in the Pacific.*

After the Battle of Midway the Japanese plans for conquest were severely set back. Although no longer able to use their fleet to push forward their advance, they continued to make use of it in a two-pronged attack: first against New Guinea, by attacking across the Papuan Peninsula in the eastern portion of that dense tropical island; and second in the Solomons by island hopping, establishing key tactical airfields along the way to provide air cover for the next hop.

In New Guinea, so very close to Australia, the main Aussie force was a single brigade which was garrisoned at Port Moresby the capital of Papua on the south coast and directly across the Queensland Straits. In March 1942, from Rabaul in New Britain, the Japanese initiated their offensive against the north coast of New Guinea, by landing near Lae, close to the Papuan Peninsula. General MacArthur was appointed Southwest Pacific Area Allied Commander-in-Chief (SWAPACINC) and assumed control of the now redeployed Australian troops and new divisions which were being formed. The US strength in Australia consisted of two divisions and eight air groups.

The USAAF was not idle during this period: equipped with P-39 and P-40 aircraft, the 8th and 35th Fighter Groups were committed to the aerial defense of Port Moresby. The first operational missions were flown on 30 April 1942. The 35th and 36th Fighter Squadrons, 8th Fighter Group dispatched thirteen aircraft to strafe Lae and Salamaua. The results left four P-39s lost for one Zero destroyed. By 1 June 1942 both squadrons had lost a total of twenty P-39s in combat, eight in crash landings and three destroyed on the ground. These units were beefed up in July by the arrival of the 80th Fighter Squadron.

In the beginning of May 1942 a

Above: *Troops of the 145th Infantry enter the ravaged Intramuros section of Manila as they pass the Post Office on the banks of the Pasig.*
Left: *B-24s on a bombing mission over the Philippines.*
Below: *Unloading supplies for a fighter group from Douglas C-47s at Finschhafen in Northeast New Guinea in December 1943.*

sizeable naval force was dispatched to seize Port Moresby and secure eastern New Guinea. It was discovered in time and intercepted by a US naval carrier force, supported by some USAAF land-based aircraft; thus the Battle of the Coral Sea began. The Japanese invasion force, especially its aircraft carriers, was sufficiently deterred to give up the planned invasion. On 2 June the 39th and 40th Fighter Squadrons, 35th Fighter Group flew their first P-40 mission. The 41st Fighter Squadron was committed in July. By 20 July the 40th had lost thirteen pilots in enemy action. Things were getting hot, and they were going to get a lot hotter.

On the 21 July the Japanese threat revived when word reached the Allies that a Japanese landing had taken place near Buna. This force of 2000 was to be used against Port Moresby in a new offensive overland. A further shock for the Allies occurred, on 29 July, when Kokoda fell, nearly halfway across the peninsula. In taking the next step, the Japanese met their master. The trail had to cross the 8500ft high Owen Stanley Mountain Range, where supplying troops became a nightmare. Within 30 days, the Japanese advance had come to a grinding halt, 34 miles from its objective.

As the USAAF units were fighting for air superiority over New Guinea and Papua, the Japanese advance had reached its zenith. On mainland Asia they had reached the border of India. In the Pacific their successes were considerable: the Philippines, the Dutch East Indies and all the primary islands north of Australia, except New

Above: *North American B-25s en route to Rabaul.*

Guinea. The Allies themselves went on the offensive on 8 August 1942 in the Solomons. The US Marines made an exceptional amphibious landing on Guadalcanal, just prior to the Japanese engineers completing an important tactical airstrip. The Marines fighting for 'the canal' as it became known, renamed the airstrip Henderson Field. It took six months of intense and bloody fighting before the Japanese finally capitulated. On 23 September the Japanese advance across the Papuan Peninsula against Port Moresby was brought to a halt.

Below: *Gunners of the 805th Engineer Aviation Battalion.*

During the summer of 1942, the few USAAF aircraft and airmen in Australia and New Guinea were doing the impossible: supporting defensive operations, eliminating Japanese logistic support of their New Guinea offensive and standing ready to meet Japanese air raids aimed at Darwin and Port Moresby. On 4 August 1942 Major General George C Kenney was named Allied Air Forces Commander in the Southwest Pacific Area.

The actual number of aircraft under Kenney's command was 245 fighters, 36 transports, 53 light bombers, 70 medium bombers and 62 heavy bombers; a total of 466 aircraft. The problem was that only 75 fighters, 16 transports, 37 medium bombers and 43 heavy bombers were combat-ready – less than 40 percent of the entire force. It was this ragtailed, undermanned and undersupplied outfit that was to become the 5th United States Air Force. Before the end of the war it would be one of the most famous of the Pacific numbered air forces. The 5th consisted of seven groups and 23 squadrons ready for combat duty.

Early October saw the Allied troops push the Japanese back across the Owen Stanley Range to the Buna-Gona beachhead; this operation was given massive air support by USAAF fighters. The new A-20s struck all along the jungle trails, flying from six new airfields near Port Moresby. (The names of these airfields were quite interesting, Seven Mile Airfield and Thirty Mile Airfield, so named because of the distance from the port.)

The 374th Troop Carrier Group was activated on 12 November and immediately started lifting Australian and US forces from Port Moresby to

Wanigela on the north coast of New Guinea. The Australian and US ground forces which were moving on Buna relied heavily on the troop carrier aircraft for supplies. The USAAF was supplying all ground forces in New Guinea due to the lack of amphibious units in the area, and the inability of the US Navy to operate in uncharted waters off the north coast of New Guinea. These transports were just as important as fighters or bombers; without them thousands of pounds of food, clothing and ammunition would not have reached the combat troops.

The next step in the jungle operations was the establishment of 'air heads', that is terminal landing fields where aircraft could unload directly into storage areas. This was urgently required as the air drops could only meet immediate needs. Numerous 'air heads' came into being, not only for supply complexes but also evacuation centers for wounded personnel. The evacuation of casualties from the front was so proficient that during the rest of the war several troop carriers were assigned to this task.

As the Allies prepared for the *coup de grâce* on Buna-Gona, USAAF aircraft maintained the isolation of the battlefield and provided maximum close-in ground support. Various tactics were developed calling for the utilization of all available aircraft to meet demands for air strikes, on a priority basis.

Shipping had first priority since Japanese reinforcement of the Buna-Gona area could only be affected by naval movement. Ground support was given secondary priority. One strike force of aircraft was on continuous ground alert, waiting for reconnaissance reports of shipping targets. As soon as the reports came in the alert force struck its targets. If there were no primary shipping targets available, they hit ground targets.

The key factor in achieving victory in the Papua Campaign was long-range aerial reconnaissance. It revealed enemy concentration, movements and new installations in adequate time for Allied forces to prepare for new offensives. Without the reconnaissance missions, flown on the most part by members of the 435th Squadron, 19th Bombardment Group, utilizing B-17Es, the success of the campaign would have been in doubt.

On 9 December 1942 the Australians captured Gona and on 14 December, US forces took Buna. At this point the northeastern port of New Guinea was secure, the airfield at Dobodura was being completed so that the Owen Stanley Range was eliminated as an obstacle. Dobodura airfield had better weather and the strike distance would be shortened.

By the end of December 1942, a two-pronged Allied offensive was taking shape. Southwest Pacific forces were moving northwest up the coast of New Guinea from the Buna-Gona area, to secure a foothold on western New Britain, and eventually advanced into the Admiralties. The South Pacific force was fighting to secure Guadalcanal and then scheduled to move on Rabaul. Rabaul, on eastern New Britains was the main Japanese strong point in the southwest Pacific, and had been under constant attack since April 1942. On 9 October 5th Bomber Command B-17s dropped 54 tons of bombs on Rabaul alone. Following this raid, on 13 October, fifteen B-17s dropped a further 30 tons on Lakunai and Vunakanua airfields. This constant pressure was applied through to the end of 1942, and culminated in thirteen attacks against Rabaul during January 1943. On 5 January two B-17s were destroyed, one taking Brigadier General Kenneth Walker, Commander of 5th Bomber Command, to his death. The loss of Walker was a blow to his command, as he was a superb leader, organizer and planner.

By the end of February the USAAF had 350 operational aircraft, one-third of which were B-17s, 43rd Bombard-

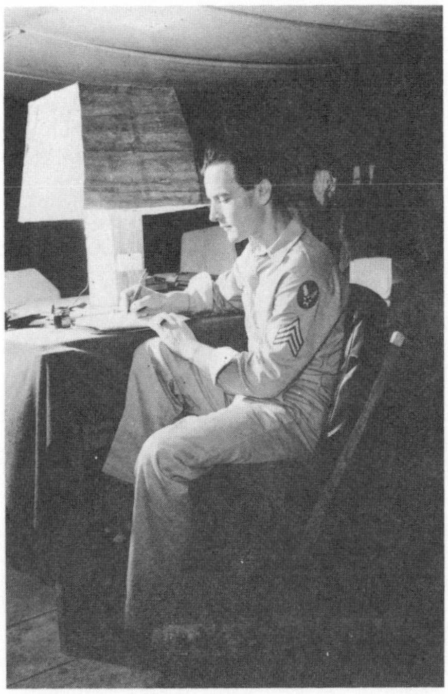

Above: *Sgt Jerry O'Neal made his lampshade from banana leaves and his chair from tail-fin cases and the frame of an old cot.*

Below: *Saipan (in the foreground) and Tinian seen through a cloud cover.*

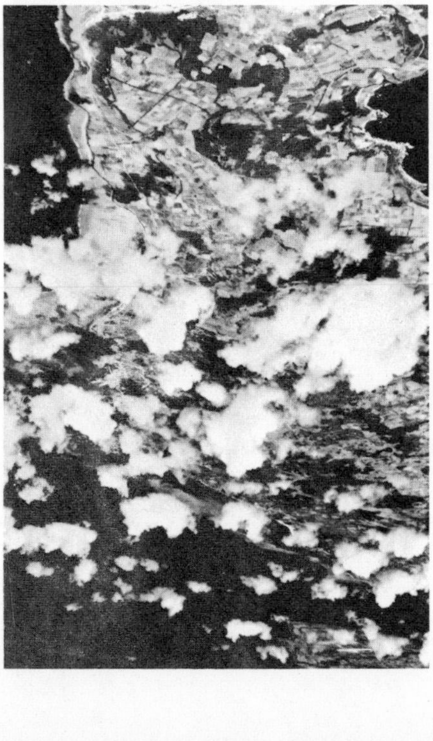

Below: *Off-duty GIs take a swim.*

ment Group and B-24s, 90th Bombardment Group. The Allies next put pressure on the Japanese bases of Lae and Salamaua. The Southwest Pacific Area forces in New Guinea were advancing on Lae and the Australians occupying Wau were only 30 miles away from Salamaua. The Aussies were counterattacked on 30 January by the Japanese, and except for the outstanding and heroic efforts of the 317th and 374th Troop Carrier Groups (TCG), the garrison would have fallen. Remarkably, these two groups flew in 948,000 lbs of troops and material.

To stop the Allied threat against Lae-Salamaua, the Japanese dispatched eight destroyers and eight transports carrying 6000 troops to Lae, on 28 February from Rabaul. These reinforcements never reached Lae. The Allies were alerted by intelligence reports, and initiated a massive reconnaissance search for this Japanese naval force. It was spotted on 1 March 1943, and the next 72 hours saw one of the most decisive air battles of the war, the Battle of the Bismarck Sea. The USAAF immediately sent fighters and light bombers to keep the Japanese fighters from supporting their support

Top left: *GIs conduct a house-to-house search at Clark Field, Luzon.*
Left: *GIs view the grim remains of some of the 117 Japanese killed when they tried to retake Aslito Field.*
Top right: *Aerial view of Maloelap Field in the Marshalls.*
Top far right: *Republic P-47 of the 7th AF on the USS* Manila Bay.
Right and below: *Liberator above Japanese-occupied Nauru Island.*

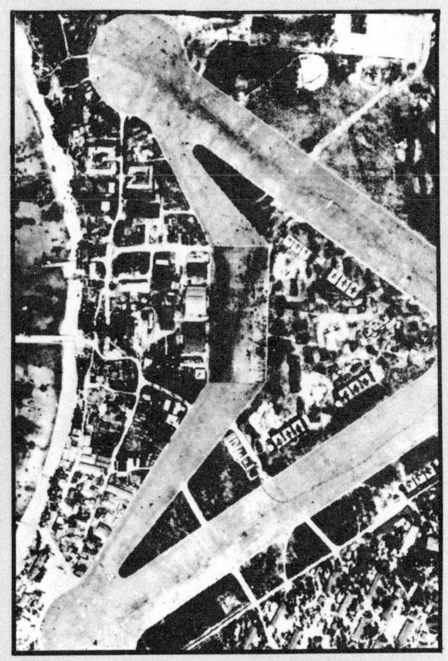

force; the rest of the Allied aircraft were dispatched to eliminate the enemy convoy.

On 2 March 28 Fortresses, 43rd Bomber Group hit the convoy sinking one transport and destroying three Zeros. However, two destroyers rescued 850 troops and successfully landed them at Lae. The decisive day was 3 March as the convoy reached Huon Gulf. The skies were clear and the weather calm. Thirteen B-17s dropped their ordnance from medium altitudes and sunk another troop transport. An aerial fight started when the Forts and their 28 P-38 escorts were hit by Zeros on escort duty. A total of twenty Zeros were claimed destroyed; one B-17 and three P-38s were lost.

Meanwhile thirteen B-25s, 38th Bombardment Group and twelve B-25Cs, 90th Bombardment Squadron came in for a low-level attack. They were followed by twelve A-20s, 89th Bombardment Squadron and six B-25s, 13th Bombardment Squadron. These attacks sunk two destroyers and three transports, and established the effectiveness of low level bombing on ships. Early that afternoon sixteen B-17s, 23 B-25s and five RAAF Bostons hit the convoy again, and sank two destroyers and two transports. The remaining transport was sunk by a naval PT-boat. Only four destroyers survived out of the sixteen-ship convoy.

On 5 March 1943 the Buna Air Task Force (BATF) was activated at Dobodura, to have first-hand control of air units. The Buna Air Task Force was redesignated the First Air Task

Above: *A Japanese guerrilla destroyed this P-47 in New Guinea.*

Right: *LST unloads on Middelburg Island off the coast of Dutch New Guinea in August 1944.*

Above: *Middleburg Island after the 836th Aviation Engineers started work on the airstrip in August 1944.*

Top: *Tents are set up near Mar Strip on Cape Sansapor on Dutch New Guinea in August 1944.*
Above: *Gasoline storage facilities were constructed on Mar Strip after the field was constructed in September 1944.*

Force, in June 1944. The Japanese operating from Rabaul and Wewak, New Guinea, concentrated on destroying the USAAF and Australian air units. From April–June, the Japanese made a total of 37 attacks on key Allied airfields. On 12 April they hit Port Moresby for the 106th time. Although one RAAF Beaufighter and three B-25s were destroyed on the ground, the combat air patrol claimed fifteen bombers and nine fighters destroyed for only two P-39s. The 54th Darwin raid occurred on 2 May 1943, and was met by three Spitfire squadrons which shot down one bomber and five Zeros saving Australia once again.

In May 1943, B-24s of the 380th Bombardment Group went operational at Darwin in Australia. This group operated against airfields, bases, industry and shipping in the Dutch East Indies, and the Banda and Timor Sea areas. Between June–August 1943, four groups became

Left: *The first US paratroops to be used in the Pacific War are dropped.*
Below: *This Zero crashed three miles south of Aitape, New Guinea.*

operational, 348th Fighter Group (P-47s), 475th Fighter Group (P-38s), 345th Bombardment Group (B-25s) and 375th Troop Carrier Group (C-47s).

On 28 July fifteen B-25 Grim Reapers hit two Japanese destroyers, the *Areake* and *Mikatsuki*, off Cape Gloucester. One destroyer was sunk and the other beached. Advances were underway on New Guinea against Lae and Salamaua; 175 tons of bombs were dropped on Salamaua on 13 August, breaking the theater bombing record.

The Japanese were still very much in the game at this time, continually raiding Allied airfields from the Wewak Area. The Wewak Area had over 2000 Japanese Army bombers and fighters based on four main airfields. The USAAF began to neutralize this threat by launching a coordinated attack at night with fragmentation clusters and incendiaries on the 17 August. Immediately after, the 32 B-25s struck in a daylight low-level attack on the same airfields. Total enemy losses claimed were 102 aircraft destroyed on the ground. These strikes

went on well into September and the Japanese never recovered.

The US strategic aim was to knock down the barriers formed by the Bismarck Archipelago, and capture Rabaul. This was to be accomplished as follows:

(1) Halsey's forces were to take the Russell Islands, west of Guadalcanal, for use as an air and naval base. Also two islands in the Trobriand group, east of New Guinea were to be seized to provide airfields for the main drive on Rabaul.

(2) Halsey would advance to New Georgia and capture Munda, a key airfield.

(3) MacArthur was to capture Lae, turn north, cross the straits to New Britain in the Bismarck Archipelago and then attack and take Rabaul.

The US advance was slow but its effect was important upon Halsey, in that he recognized the drawbacks of a step-by-step advance. By early Octo-

Above: *PFC Fuzzy Edwards of Nashville, Tennessee, keeps troops of the 24th Infantry amused during a jam session staged by the 13th Air Force.*

5th Air Forces, February 1944

780 bombers
803 fighters
173 reconnaissance
328 transports

Above: *Saipan airstrip after a Japanese air raid in November 1944.*

ber, the USAAF was heavily committed to the reduction of Rabaul. The 11 October saw Colonel Neil E Kearby, commander of the 348th Fighter Group lead four P-47s on a reconnaissance mission over Wewak. They jumped a formation of twelve Japanese bombers and 36 fighters while on patrol. Kearby attacked and shot down three Japanese Oscars and two Tonys. For this gallant action against odds of 12 to 1, he was awarded the Medal of Honor.

At the end of December 1943, the Southwest Pacific forces were prepared to invade New Britain, and Cape Gloucester was the main objective on the western tip. The 5th Air Force hit targets continuously from mid-November to the end of December. The Japanese reaction came on 26 December, when 25 bombers and 50 Zero escorts first struck at the fleet units, sinking one destroyer. The 35th and 36th Fighter Squadrons intercepted this force, resulting in one of the largest fights of the entire war. Two P-38s and two P-47s were lost for 22 Japanese bombers and 24 Zeros destroyed. The Cape Gloucester airfield was taken on 30 December, but fighting continued into the new year. During the Cape Gloucester offensive, four units received the coveted Distinguished Unit Citation (DUC): the 38th Bomber Group, 35th and 36th Fighter Squadrons and the 348th Fighter Group.

The Southwest Pacific Area forces

Below: *GI examines a wrecked Zero on Munda Island in the Solomons.*

were concentrated to advance along the north coast of New Guinea. A 500 mile jump was to be taken to Aitape and Hollandia, by-passing Wewak and Madang. The softening up of Hollandia began on 4 March 1944. Attacks were conducted against Wewak at the same time. The two leading fighter aces of the theater were killed along the New Guinea coast within five days of each other.

On 4 March Colonel Kearby led a flight of P-47s into fifteen Japanese fighters near Wewak, shot one down immediately and brought another down a few minutes later but in the ensuing battle was himself shot down. Lt Colonel Thomas J Lynch and Major Richard I Bong, 39th Fighter Squadron, flying P-38s attacked two enemy planes and Lynch shot one down. Then they attacked a corvette which resulted in Lynch's aircraft sustaining damage. He bailed out but did not have sufficient height for his parachute to open.

In the Pacific in the spring of 1944 Spruance's Central Pacific Forces had taken the Gilbert and Marshall Islands, and devastated the Japanese base of Truk in the Caroline Islands by air bombardment. MacArthur's Southwest Pacific Forces had captured the Bismarck Archipelago and the Admiralty Islands, and neutralized the Japanese base of Rabaul. MacArthur was also extending his advance westward in New Guinea in preparation for his next move, the Philippines.

During April MacArthur was pushing to capture Hollandia on Humboldt Bay, 200 miles west of Wewak. The landings were preceded by heavy air bombardment which destroyed the

Right: *Aerial view of B-25s on the Mar Strip near Cape Sansapor.*
Below: *The Owen Stanley Range.*
Below right: *P-47 Thunderbolt.*

majority of Japanese aircraft scraped together to defend the sector. By 2 May Hollandia was secure and elements of the USAAF could launch missions against the southern Philippines. In mid-May US troops landed on the New Guinea coast, and crossed over the narrow straight to Wakde Island. Wakde was secured on 18 May, and the airfield was back in operation by 22 May. His next jump was to capture Biak Island with its airfields, 350 miles west of Hollandia. Biak was the largest of the Schouten Islands and possessed three airfields. It was invaded on 27 May, followed by a massive ground offensive. Even with 2260 tons of bombs dropped on it, the garrison did not give up till 20 June.

At an inter-service conference at Pearl Harbor in July in which MacArthur's and Nimitz's planners took part, it was agreed that a move into the southern or central Philippines should precede an invasion of Formosa or Luzon. The Joint Chiefs had also reluctantly come to the same conclusion. MacArthur wanted to recapture the Philippines because he had given his word to the Filipino people and he intended to keep it. The mopping up program in New Guinea was progressing as rapidly as possible. He decided to allow both the Army and Navy to take the Philippines jointly and did not want to waste any time, especially with Nimitz racing towards the Philippines. During the meeting with Roosevelt in Hawaii in late July, he saw how General Robert C Richardson was outgunned by the Navy in Nimitz's theater. Leahy, King, Nimitz and Halsey were present so it took MacArthur a long time to put his points across.

In September it was decided to forego Formosa in favor of Luzon. The Leyte decision made it feasible to attack Luzon two months early. Furthermore the Japanese offensive in China threatened to overrun US airfields and these airfields could be used to support an assault on Formosa. The USAAF units in the Pacific were becoming less manageable as they 'island hopped' further afield. The result was the establishment of a new Far East Air Force on 15 June 1944, commanded by General Kenney. All numbered air forces in the Pacific now came under Kenney's control. Kenney appointed Lt General Enis Whitehead, his able deputy, as commander of the 5th. The 13th was commanded by Major General St Clair Street. The close Kenney–Whitehead relationship meant that the 5th would be chosen as the principal air assault force for MacArthur's operations for the rest of the war. Street's 13th Air Force was placed in a supporting role. However all was not 'milk and honey' between the air force commanders, Whitehead and Street, who were constantly at each other's throats.

MacArthur lost no time when his Biak advance was slowed down; he mounted an immediate attack on Noemfoor Island. The island was taken on 6 July and all three of its airfields were back in operation soon afterwards. The Japanese had no air strength left; the remaining troops on the mainland had already given up or moved to the western portion of the Vogelkop Peninsula. On 30 July MacArthur put a division ashore near Cape Sansapor, set up a defensive zone and started to build airfields. The way was now clear for the next leap, the Philippines.

MacArthur needed pre-invasion mapping of the Philippines and the 6th Reconnaissance Group was ordered

Below: *Makeshift 'Java Gadget' served as a giant coffee pot, made from two oxygen tanks.*

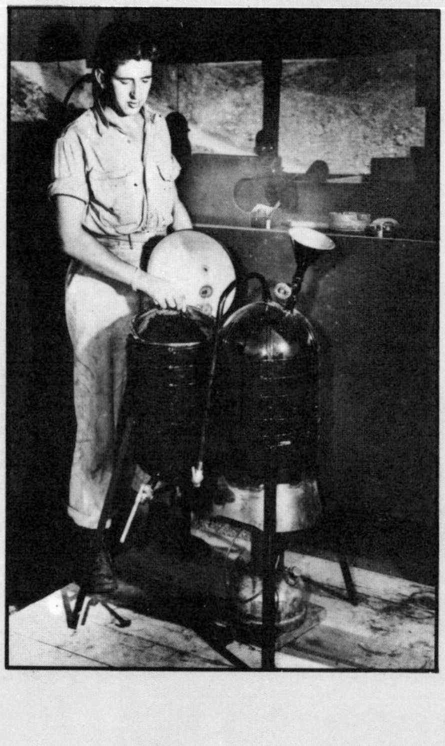

Below: *The 'Sweetheart of Bougainville' carved out of wood by TSgt R H Harris.*

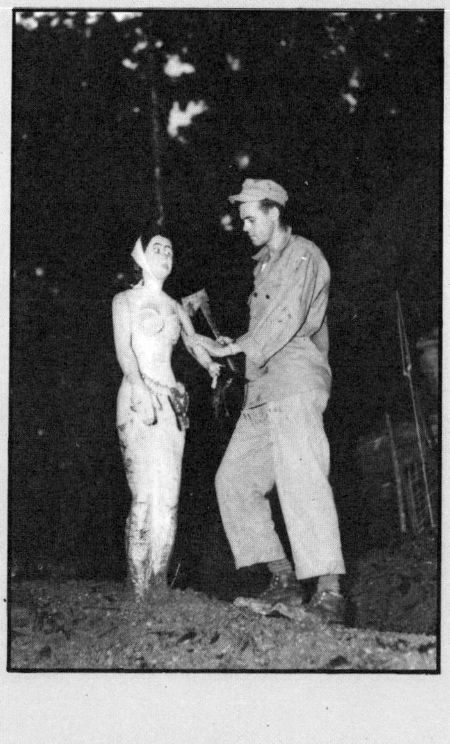

Left: *Tight formation of a P-47, P-38 and P-51 over Iwo Jima.*

Below: *Corregidor, seen from the bomb-bay of the 22nd Bomb Group, 1945.*
Bottom: *B-24 strikes Corregidor prior to the retaking of the island.*

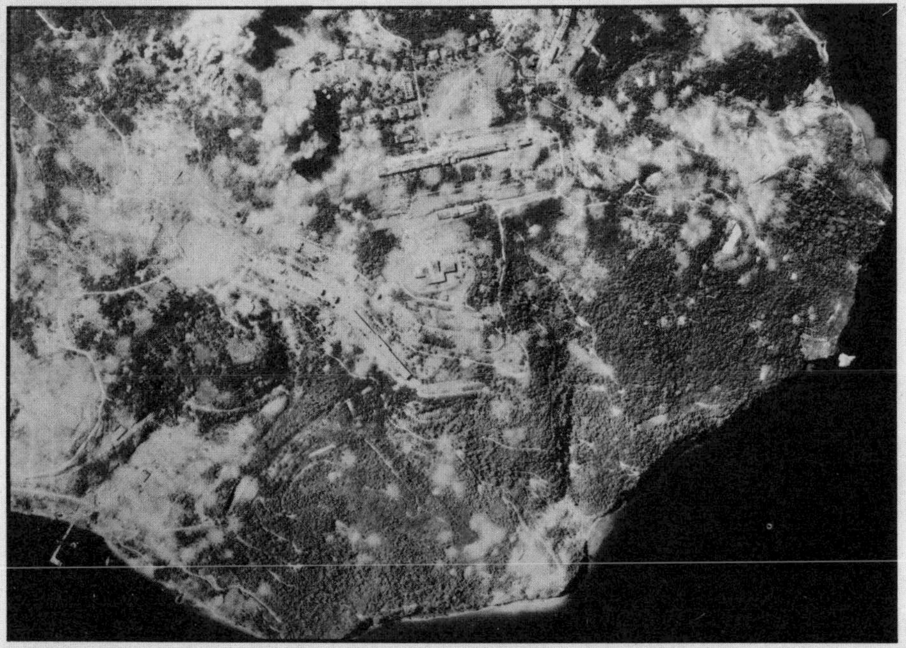

to get it. This group flew, 1530-mile unescorted roundtrips for an entire week in September to obtain the required priority photographs despite hazardous weather. Finally the capture of Morotai and the Palaus provided the advanced bases necessary for the assault on the Philippines. It was believed that the Japanese air strength in the Philippines was very weak and their naval forces would not be able to respond in time. The 5th Air Force was to neutralize enemy air forces on Mindanao, guard convoys and cover the western flank until relieved by the 13th Air Force.

Leyte consisted of mountainous terrain, except for the two plains in the north, the Leyte Valley and the Ormoc Valley. MacArthur planned to build large air and logistical bases in these plains to support future operations. Whitehead's 5th was to give air support, but Halsey's and Kinkaid's carrier aircraft carried the brunt of the pre-invasion raids. During this phase, 5th and 13th Air Forces were to neutralize enemy air and naval units within range of USAAF bases at Morotai and Vogelkop. In fact, this was a joint operation because all three Allied Theaters would be cooperating with SWPA Theater's invasion of Leyte: Mountbatten's Southeast Asia Command, Nimitz's Pacific Ocean Theater and Stilwell's CBI. The invasion of Leyte occurred on 20 October 1944 on the east coast, near Dulag and Tacloban where the US 6th Army landed. The Japanese launched a massive Combined Fleet operation to stop the landings on 23 October. Then, the US forces expanding on both flanks threw the Japanese into total disarray; the Battle of Leyte Gulf was now in full swing. The Japanese lost three battleships, including the 18in gun

Musashi, all four carriers, six heavy and four light cruisers, and nine destroyers. The US forces lost one carrier, two escort carriers, one destroyer and two destroyer escorts.

Although heavy tropical rains and swamp-like conditions prevailed, an airstrip was established at Tacloban. At the end of October, P-38s of the 49th Fighter Group were flying missions in support of ground operations. In 45 days, the 49th flew 2468 sorties and shot down 132 enemy aircraft. On 7 December, in an effort to secure Leyte quickly, a US amphibious force landed at Ormoc. At practically the same time, the Japanese attempted to land a brigade close by. Both forces were supported by air cover which resulted in quite a battle. The entire Japanese convoy was destroyed and one US destroyer and one transport were sunk by suicide attacks. The 49th and 475th Fighter Groups claimed 53 downed enemy aircraft for the loss of one plane. Ground fighting continued on Leyte until 8 May 1945, but MacArthur went ahead with his plans for Luzon. By 15 December Mindoro was invaded. This was a risky move as Mindoro was only 300 miles from Leyte Gulf and much closer to Luzon, and its Japanese airfields. The Japanese garrison had only 100 men, and the four Japanese airfields were occupied within three hours of the landing.

The largest single coordinated mission was flown on 7 January 1945 against Clark Field. The results included 60 enemy aircraft destroyed on the ground. The attacking US light and medium bombers lost one B-25 and four A-20s. But this day saw the loss of Major Thomas B McGuire Jr who crashed in his P-38 while attempting to destroy an Oscar. He was awarded the Medal of Honor for downing seven enemy fighters on 25–26 December, bringing his total to 38 victories.

Below: *The wreckage of the Intramuros (walled city) part of Manila.*

The 7th Army invaded Luzon, on 9 January 1945, at Lingayen Gulf. By the middle of January, USAAF units began to secure air space over Luzon. Manila was taken on 3 February; the next step was to retake Bataan and Corregidor. Bataan fell on 20 February and Corregidor on the 27 February. Resistance in Luzon had ended by 1 July 1945. The Luzon campaign was the largest and bloodiest fought by MacArthur's forces in the southwest Pacific. In seven months of ruthless fighting, 8300 Americans, 1100 Filipinos and 205,000 Japanese were killed. Yamashita and his troops effected a substantial delaying action but in the end General Krueger had conquered the largest Japanese Army in the Pacific.

Now the USAAF was committed to a major target, Formosa, with its 53 airfields and numerous ports. The first attacks were flown at night by B-24s, 63rd Bomber Squadron on 11 January 1945. The first daylight raid was conducted on 22 July by the 22nd Bomber Group, escorted by the 8th and 43rd Fighter Groups. By April only 100 Japanese remained out of the original 600 on Formosa. Airfields, ports, power plants, sugar mills and alcohol plants were devastated in turn.

Finally, by early July, Formosa was in tatters and its ports closed. Total sorties flown against Formosa were 5000 B-24s, 1400 B-25s and over 1000 fighters. Over 15,315 tons of bombs were dropped on Formosan targets. Attacks on shipping were made by night-flying B-24s and B-25s. On 5 April three 3rd Bomber Group A-20s rigged with an additional wing tank, led by Colonel Richard E Ellis hit a Hong Kong convoy. Ellis sent a 2193 ton cargo-ship to the bottom.

The USAAF proved itself invaluable in the Pacific just as its European counterpart had. The next major step was the total commitment of the 5th, 7th, 13th and 20th Air Forces to neutralize Japan prior to the planned invasion.

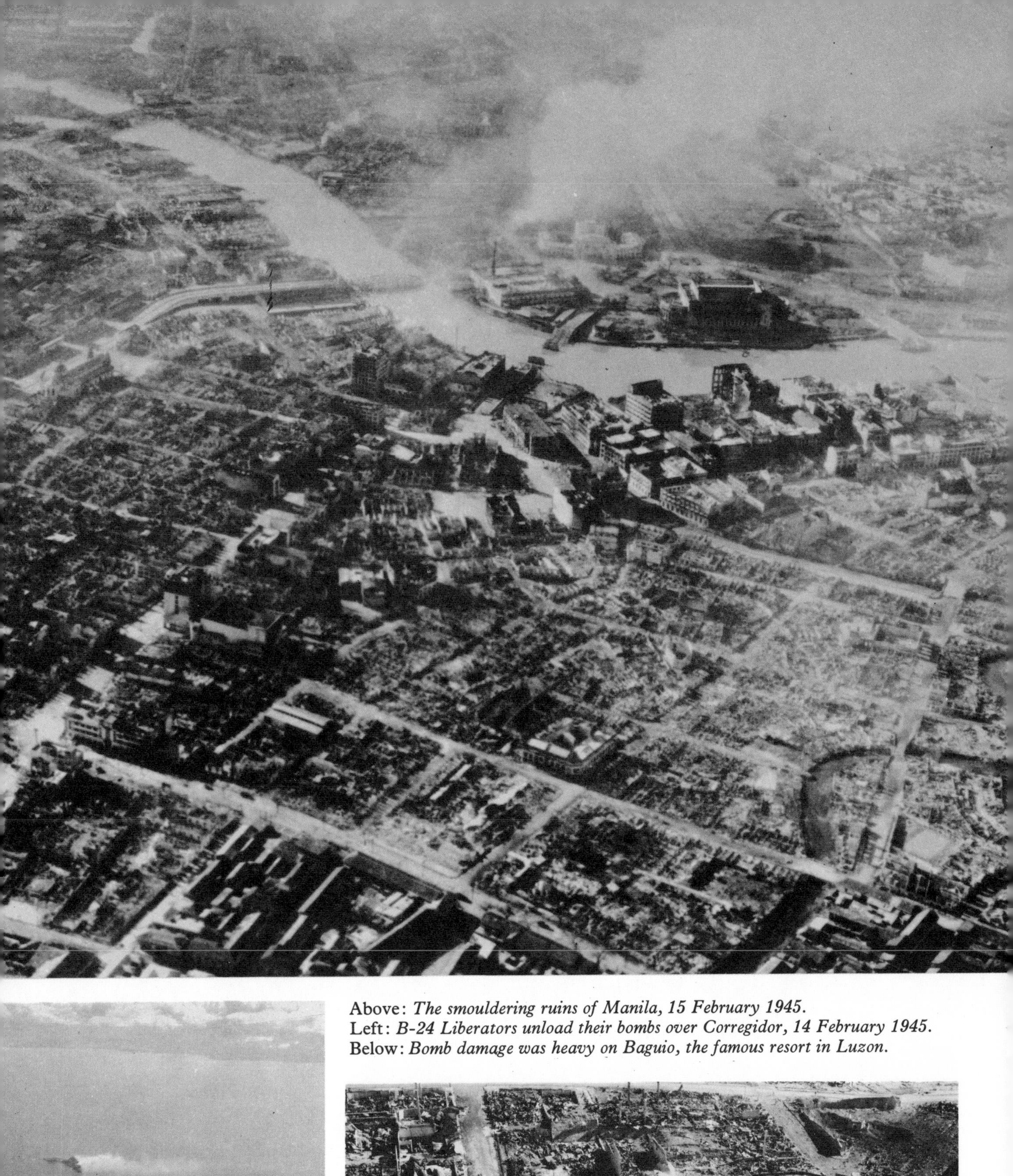

Above: *The smouldering ruins of Manila, 15 February 1945.*
Left: *B-24 Liberators unload their bombs over Corregidor, 14 February 1945.*
Below: *Bomb damage was heavy on Baguio, the famous resort in Luzon.*

Over the Reich

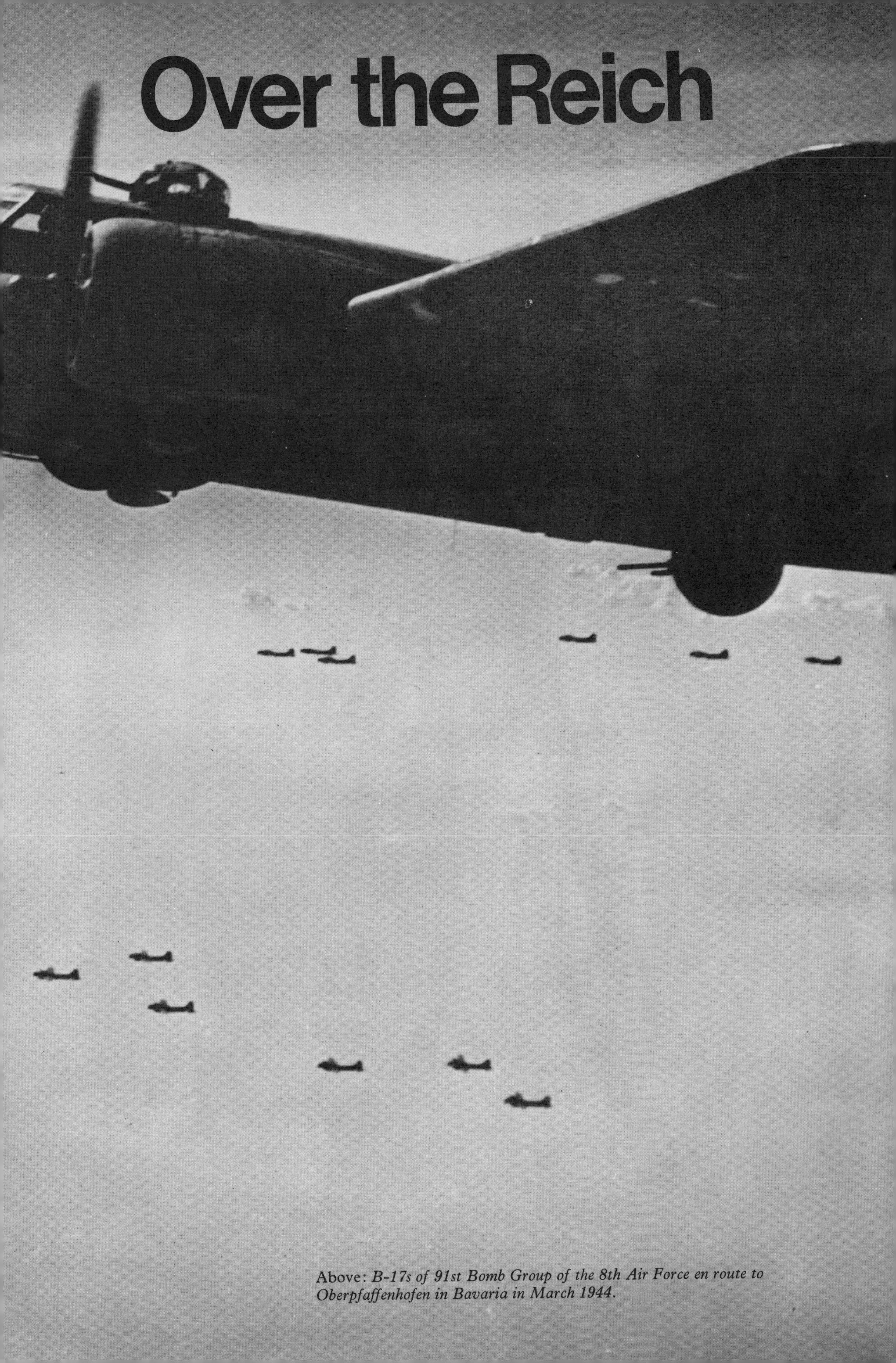

Above: *B-17s of 91st Bomb Group of the 8th Air Force en route to Oberpfaffenhofen in Bavaria in March 1944.*

With bad weather throughout the winter, the 8th Air Force had been hampered in its desire to strike hard against priority targets in Germany. But the break finally came on 19 February 1944, when an extensive high pressure area moving across Central Germany brought clear blue skies. This was a heaven-sent opportunity for the generals of USSTAF. Now was the chance to launch the long-planned concentrated strikes against German air industries which were high on the priority list.

On 20 February 1944, a cold and blustery Sunday morning, over one thousand bombers were sent against twelve critical targets in Germany. This force consisted of ten combat wings, and was supported by all available long-range fighters. Losses were very light; only 21 bombers were lost. The mission itself was highly successful with considerable damage recorded on the aircraft complexes attacked. The 20 February also saw three Medals of Honor awarded to men of the 8th Air Force. One bomber of the 305th Bombardment Group turning away from its target ran head-on into a section of enemy fighters. The pilot, 1st Lt Bill Lawley, was seriously wounded, and the engine was on fire. Lawley, acting coolly, brought the aircraft out of its dive and ordered the crew to evacuate the damaged aircraft. The crew all stayed on board. The fire was put out and the aircraft headed for England, when they were hit again by enemy fighters and another engine caught fire. Lawley took evasive action, managing to lose the fighters and put out the fire. The aircraft was finally brought back to the nearest airfield at Redhill on only one engine and a prayer. The other two men to receive Medals of Honor (posthumously) were Lt Walter Truemper and Sgt Archie Mathis, of the 351 Bomber Group who died attempting to bring in their severely damaged aircraft at Polebrook.

The 19–25 February 1944 showed the heaviest concentration of attacks made by the 8th Air Force – no wonder it was referred to as 'Big Week'. The damage to aircraft factories at Fürth, Regensburg and Stuttgart deprived the Luftwaffe of badly needed fighters. The 8th Air Force was the single largest air force at the conclusion of the campaign. The USSTAF was visibly drawing tight strings around Germany; the ring was starting to close. The next step was D-Day.

At the Arcadia Conference in Washington in December 1941, Winston Churchill proposed an Anglo-American invasion of North Africa as the first step in 'closing the ring' on Hitler's Reich. This was to be followed up in the spring of 1943 by landings on the west coast of France. Churchill had always been Mediterranean-oriented ever since World War I and the ill-fated Gallipoli assault. The primary reason why US planners favored an early invasion of Europe was to succor Russia. The Russian Red Army's firm resistance to Hitler reinforced the strategy of a 'Germany first' decision. Besides, if Hitler defeated Russia, it would have the gravest implications for the Allies. Over 40 crack Wehrmacht divisions could be redeployed to the Western Front. This was the background to Overlord, the invasion of western France.

At the start of 1944 the United States Strategic Air Forces in Europe (USSTAF), was established, with operational control of both the 8th and 15th Air Forces. Preparations for D-Day, codenamed Operation Overlord, were well underway and the proposed date, weather permitting, would be early June 1944. Success in the Mediterranean, in the Atlantic and on the eastern front was clearly evident. The ring was drawing tighter and tighter around Germany.

Twenty-three German divisions were being held in Italy, although Field Marshal Kesselring's excellent leadership at Anzio and Monte Cassino prevented the Allies from advancing until mid-1944. The Russian armies were breaking out through a salient west of Kiev and had passed the upper Prut by May. The Yugoslav partisans under Tito were diverting even more German troops. The time was ripe for an Allied initiative against western Europe, namely, the recovery of France and the opening of a second front to alleviate some of the pressure on the Russians.

The United States Strategic Air Forces in Europe, commanded by

Above: *GIs of the 101st Airborne Division's 327th Glider Infantry Regiment view the Bavarian Alps.*

Below: *Swing band of the 381st Bomb Group plays a dance at the Aero Club.*

Above: *Bob Hope, Capt Billy Southworth and Col C A Marion.*

Above: *GIs of the 401st Bomb Group enjoying a Red Cross dance given at their Aero Club in February 1944.*

General Spaatz played a major if not decisive role in the reconquest of western Europe. The 8th Air Force under General Doolittle was hitting aircraft factories and oil targets. In fact, the summer months saw the 8th and 15th Air Forces exert their maximum strength against the German war economy. The 8th alone dropped over 36,000 tons in May, 60,000 tons in June, 45,000 tons in July and over 49,000 tons in August for a grand total of 190,000 tons over a four-month period.

The 6 June 1944 saw General Dwight D Eisenhower, Supreme Allied Commander Europe (SACEUR), give the order to launch the greatest assault force in history on the sandy beaches of Normandy. It was extremely ironic that the location of the launching of the last successful invasion of England in 1066 was now to be invaded in turn.

American planners and strategists had hoped to cross the Channel in force in 1943. But with Rommel driven out of North Africa, and Sicily there for the taking, the Allies continued to advance. The Allies finally did agree to attempt a cross-Channel invasion, in May 1944, Sir Frederick Morgan, Chief of Staff, SACEUR, was the man selected to initiate a plan for the proposed invasion. The codename was

Below: *Bombers are checked on the flight line in southern Holland in 1945.*

Top: *Generals Auton, Eisenhower, Spaatz, Doolittle, Kepner and Col Blakelle at an award ceremony in England.*
Above: *The first American baseball game played at Eton College in July 1944.*
Right: *The remains of the Zeiss optical equipment factory in Jena.*

Overlord. Not until the Teheran Conference, did Roosevelt, Churchill and Stalin choose the leaders to launch the second front.

SACEUR: General Dwight D Eisenhower
Deputy Commander SACEUR: Sir Arthur Tedder
Chief of Staff: Major General Walter Bedell Smith
Commander British–Canadian Force: General Bernard L Montgomery
Commander US Force: General Omar N Bradley
CINC Allied Navy: Sir Bertram Ramsay
Allied Air Force: Sir Trafford Leigh-Mallory

As the Allied Chiefs planned the coming invasion, the strategic bomber forces changed their strikes from targets deep in Europe to areas related to the actual landings. This was to make the sending of German reinforcements to the landing areas virtually impossible. The 8th Air Force struck bridges across the Seine, marshaling yards, coastal defenses, and numerous transportation facilities.

The success of the Normandy landings insured the unconditional surrender of Germany. The issue was no longer in doubt. The Germans continued to fight but it was a losing battle. The pre-invasion softening-up started on 2 June, when the 8th launched strike after strike against transportation centers and airfields in northern France, and hit coastal defenses extremely hard, especially in the Pas de Calais section. This was all part of Operation Cover to deceive the Germans as to where the actual invasion would occur. The first mission consisted of 776 B-17s and B-24s attacking targets at Boulogne-sur-Mer, Vannes, Equihem-Plage, Hardelot-Plage, Neufchâteau and Saint Aubin. The Luftwaffe opposition was totally ineffective. The 8th followed up with an immediate second mission striking airfields and railroad

Right: *B-24 Liberator is shot down over Germany in February 1944.*
Far right: *Ludwigshafen chemical and oil production factories were leveled by constant bombing attacks.*

facilities at Conches, Achères, Paris, Creil, Brétigny-sur-Orne and Juvisy-sur-Orne. The mission was quite successful; out of 300 heavies dispatched, only eight were lost to AA fire.

This constant pre-invasion softening-up continued through to 5 June. The P-38s of the 8th and 9th Air Forces were to provide air cover for the Allied invasion fleet in the Channel under Admiral Sir Bertram Ramsay. The P-47s and P-51s of the 8th were to provide high altitude cover for the bomber force and troop carriers, and to destroy any enemy aircraft attempting to reach the landing beaches. At 1255 hours, 6 June 1944, the first P-51s were taking off from their English bases to start their patrols. Luftwaffe opposition was expected to be extremely tough once the invasion was fully discovered by the German High Command, but this threat never materialized.

The 8th flew four missions in support of Overlord; 1361 heavy bombers were dispatched on the first mission alone to attack beach installations and bomb transportation checkpoints in Caen. The second mission struck at transportation facilities in towns immediately near the assault areas. Cloud coverage caused most of the 520 bombers to return but 37 managed to drop their bombs on the secondary target of Argentan. The third mission was against the important communications center of Caen. The fourth mission was a general follow-up, striking primarily at towns south and east of the assault areas. The 8th dropped over 3596 tons of bombs from 1729 heavy bombers during D-Day, with only three losses.

Meanwhile, more than 800 A-20s and B-26s of the 9th Air Force, attacked coastal batteries, rail and road junctions in support of the invasion. Over 2000 fighters flew sweeps over the fleet and assault beaches, and a further 1400 troop carriers delivered troops and paratroops including three fully airborne divisions, to secure beachheads and to facilitate movement of seaborne assault forces. Thirty aircraft were lost during the invasion.

The day selected for the invasion was 5 June 1944, the day when the Allies would start the ball rolling to free Western Europe from the dominating clutches of its German conquerors. All strategic and tactical air units were prepared for their own individual assignments, and the troop carrier groups were ready to move men, equipment and gliders to predesignated landing zones (LZs). These landing zones were along the northern

Left: *Bing Crosby entertains more than 4000 8th AF men.*

Above: *B-24 Liberator* Umbriago, *named after one of Jimmy Durante's imaginary characters, on a mission to Saarbrücken in July 1944.*
Left: *The ruins of Goebbels' Propaganda Ministry in Berlin. In the foreground German citizens take wood to their dwellings.*
Below left: *POW's await evacuation from Moosburg in May 1945.*
Below: *Officers of the 654th Bomb Squadron of the 25th Bomb Group stand beside a flak-damaged Mosquito in England.*

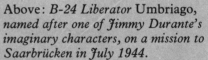

North American P-51D Mustang

The marriage of a highly advanced airframe with a license-built version of the Rolls-Royce Merlin engine, which had enabled the Hurricane and Spitfire fighters of the RAF to win the Battle of Britain, gave the USAAF its finest fighter of World War II. P-51B Mustangs, first of the Merlin-powered models, began escorting bombers of the US 8th Air Force over Europe in December 1943. The P-51D of 1944 introduced a new blister canopy, giving the pilot an all-round view. With two long-range jettisonable fuel tanks under its wings, it could escort the B-17s and B-24s all the way to Berlin. Goering is supposed to have commented he knew the war was lost for Germany when he saw the first Mustangs over the capital. In less than two years of fighting over Europe, they claimed the destruction of 4950 Luftwaffe aircraft in the air, and 4131 on the ground, for the loss of 2520 Mustangs in combat.

The P-51D spanned 37ft, was 32ft 3in long, was powered by a 1490 hp Packard-built V-1650-7 (Merlin) engine, and weighed 11600 lb fully loaded. Armament comprised six 0.50 in machine guns mounted in the wings, with provision for a pair of 1000-lb bombs for ground attack missions. Maximum speed was 437 mph at 25,000ft, and range anything up to 2000 miles with underwing tanks.

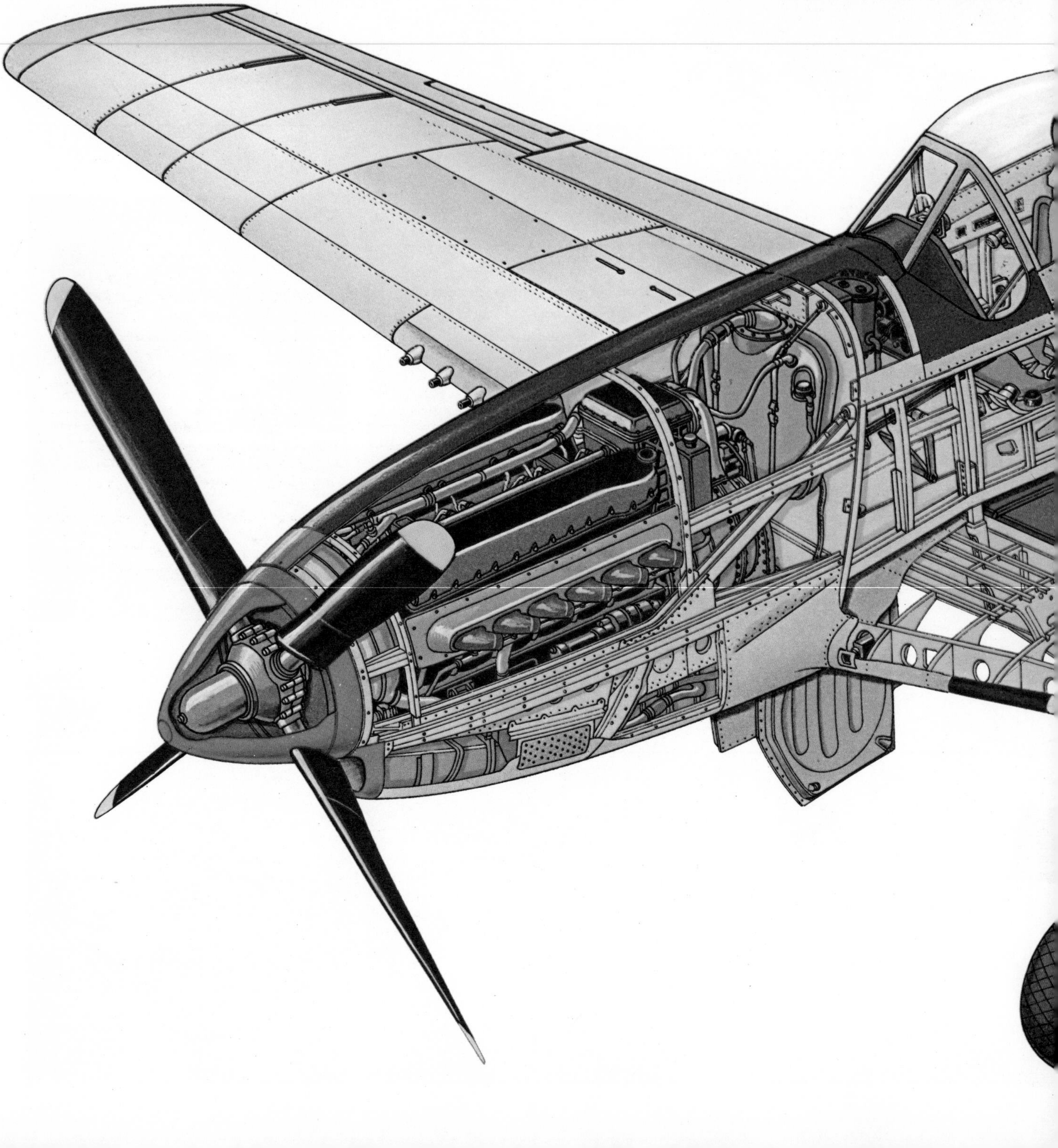

Left: *Armorers of the 45th Fighter Squadron based on Saipan load ammunition on a P-51 before take-off for Iwo Jima.*

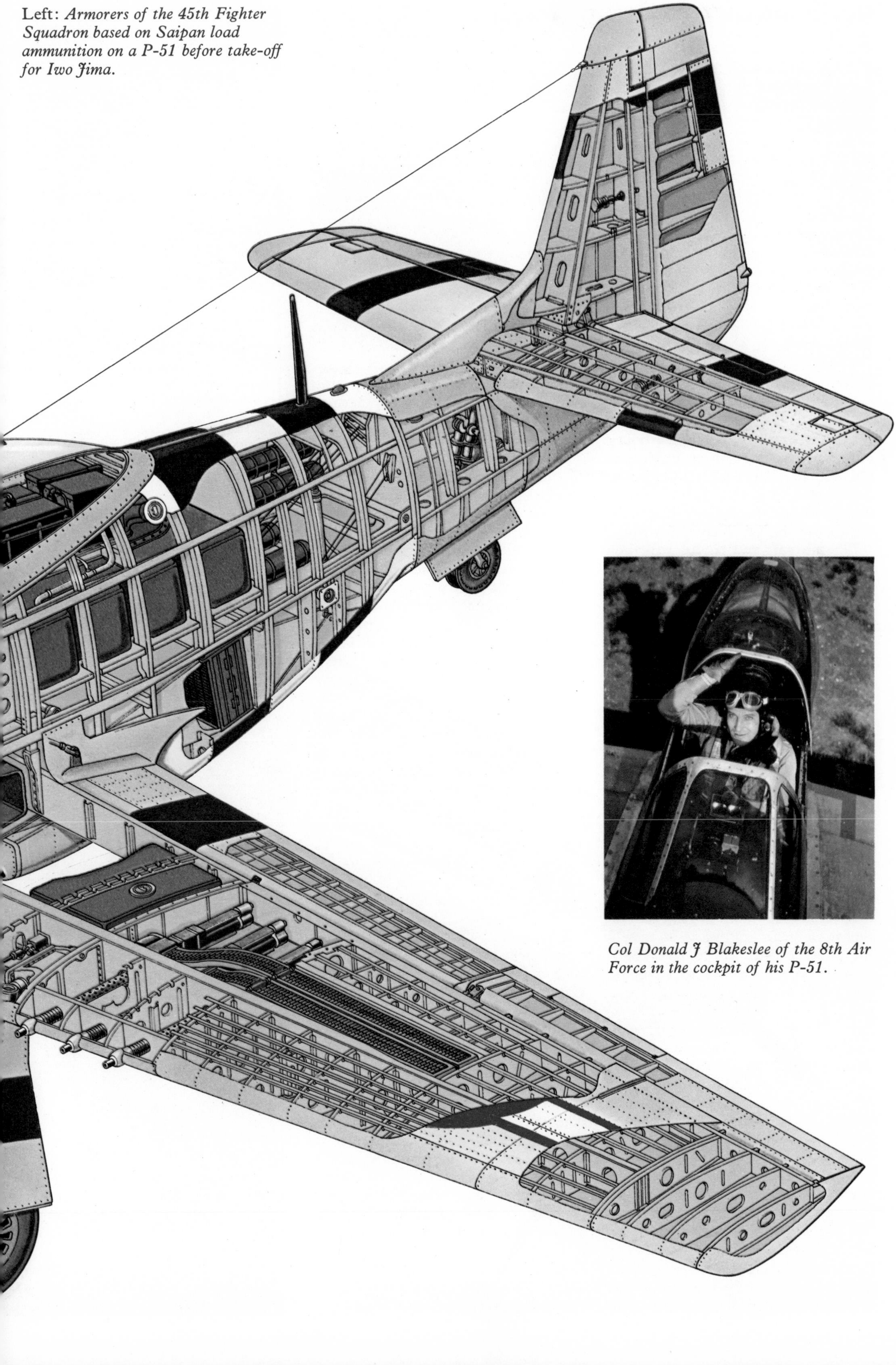

Col Donald J Blakeslee of the 8th Air Force in the cockpit of his P-51.

Above: *German vehicles and horses surrender in France in May 1945.*

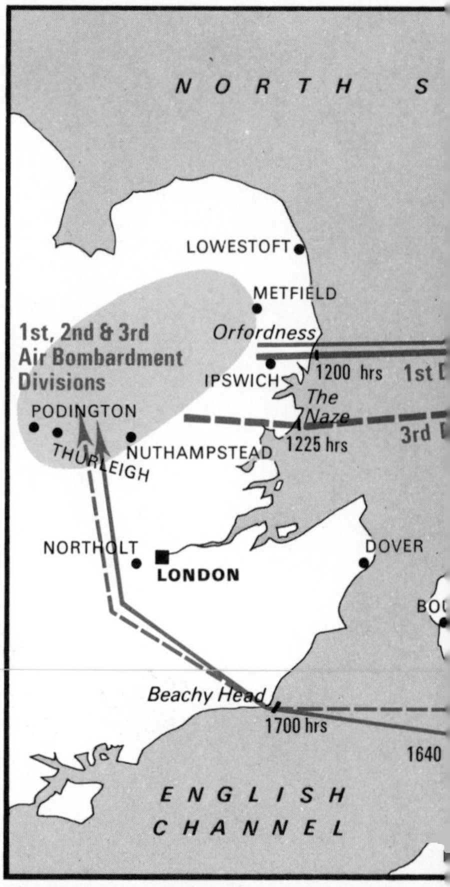

coast of Normandy, east of Cherbourg, and between Ste Mère Eglise and Ouistreham. The five beachheads were codenamed: Omaha, Utah, US 1st Army, Gold, Juno, Sword, British 2nd Army and Canadian 1st Army.

The aircraft and troops were now ready to go, but as usual the weather again turned bad on 4 June. General Eisenhower, the Supreme Allied Commander, was forced to delay the invasion. Finally, after much deliberation, he chose 6 June as the day for the invasion. Now the die was cast and the invasion on. By 5 June all Allied aircraft participating were painted with alternating black and white bands completely around the wings and fuselage, called Invasion stripes. This was accomplished to prevent a repeat of the losses sustained by the 316th Fighter Group during the Husky operation, and would identify them as friendly aircraft.

Brigadier General Paul L William's 9th Troop Carrier Command was to drop the 82nd and 101st Airborne Divisions on six landing zones close to Ste Mère Eglise. There crack paratroops were to seize bridges, key points and roads to assist the speedy movement of troops from the beaches inland. These C-47s and C-53s were leaving from transport bases such as Aldermaston, Welford, Greenham Common, Saltby and Stanehoe. General Eisenhower told paratroops at Greenham Common, 'the eyes of the world are upon you.'

Although some errors were made, the airborne landings were a success and losses were not high. Of 821 troop carriers dispatched, only 21 were lost; and out of 104 gliders and tugs, only two tugs were lost. The 101st Airborne (Screaming Eagles) Division was dropped without a loss, while only one unit of the 82nd made a bad drop. This unit was very unlucky, dropping right into the middle of the 91st German Infantry Division, which was engaged in maneuvers.

The amphibious landings were set for 0630 hours and were covered by Allied air units. The landings were a success, and the invasion forces were consolidating beachheads while troops moved inland. By the middle of June the US 1st Army; consisting of nine divisions, had thrust up the Cherbourg peninsula to within a few miles of Valognes. The US 7th Corps broke through the German lines and sealed off the Cotentin peninsula and Cherbourg by 17 June. The USAAF pilots, who flew close-in ground support during this critical period, not only had to contend with a cornered enemy, but with trigger-happy Allied gunners as well. By mid-July the US 1st Army had established a line running from St Lô to the west coast of Normandy, and had now encountered stubborn German resistance along the eastern sectors. The heavy concentration of German troops and armor in the east dictated that a breakthrough would have its best chance in the west.

The point selected for the Allied push was St Lô beginning with a heavy air and artillery bombardment of the German lines. This joint effort was codenamed Operation Cobra. It called for massive attacks by the 8th and 9th Air Forces beginning on 25 July. The 9th attacked the area south of the St Lô, Periers road, at 0945 hours and was followed up by 1507 heavy bombers saturating the target area with over 3300 tons of bombs. This massive air assault continued until 1100 hours when the US 1st Army struck the German lines. The constant pressure of five consecutive weeks, on land and in the air, had severely

Top right: *The Schweinfurt Raids.*
Right: *B-24s of the 15th Air Force over Hungary in September 1944.*

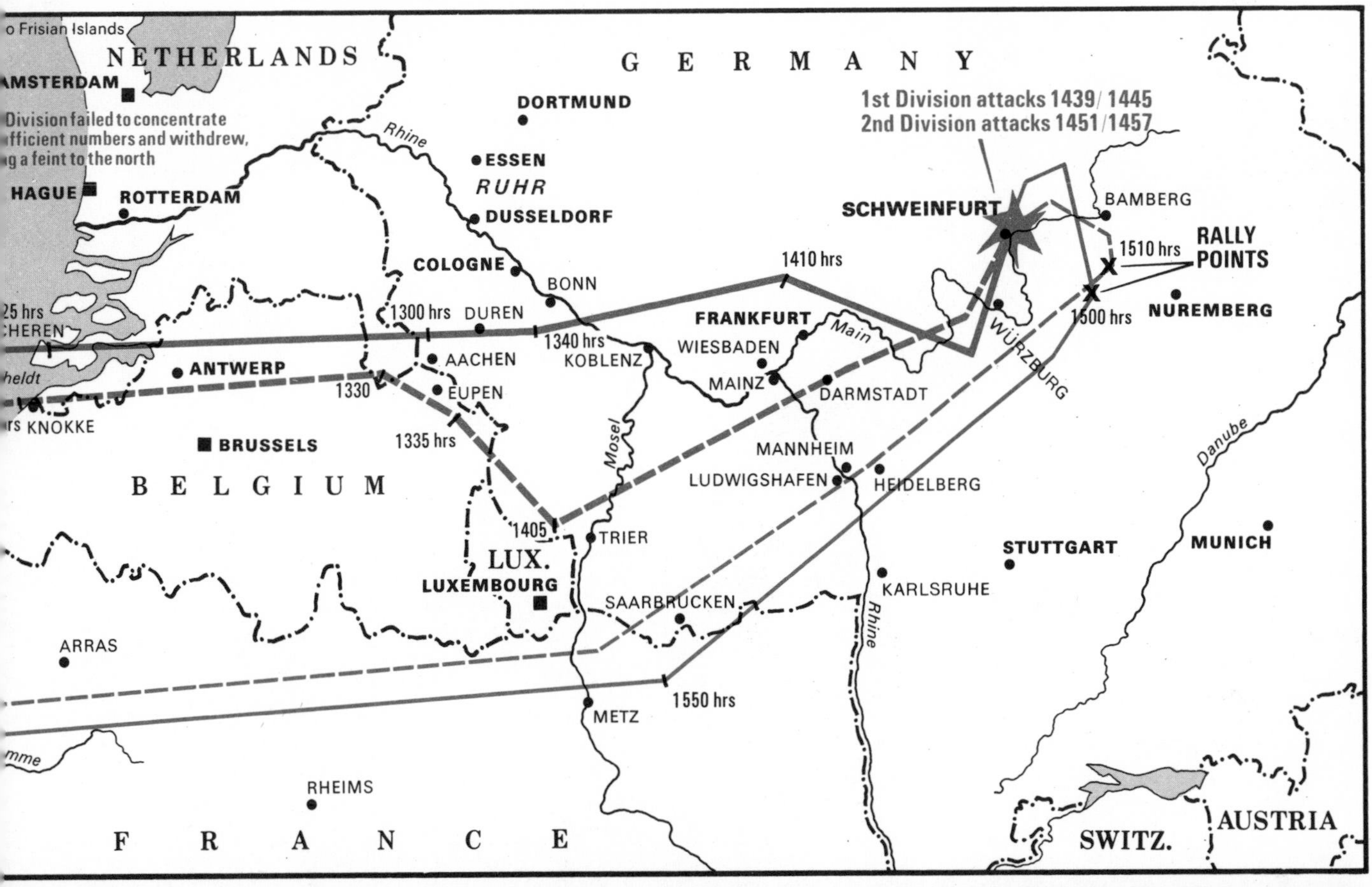
o Frisian Islands
NETHERLANDS
GERMANY
AMSTERDAM
Division failed to concentrate
fficient numbers and withdrew,
g a feint to the north
DORTMUND
1st Division attacks 1439/1445
2nd Division attacks 1451/1457
Rhine
ESSEN
RUHR
HAGUE
ROTTERDAM
DUSSELDORF
SCHWEINFURT
BAMBERG
RALLY
POINTS
1510 hrs
1410 hrs
COLOGNE
BONN
1500 hrs
NUREMBERG
25 hrs
CHEREN
1300 hrs
DUREN
FRANKFURT
Main
1340 hrs
KOBLENZ
WIESBADEN
WÜRZBURG
AACHEN
ANTWERP
1330
EUPEN
MAINZ
DARMSTADT
KNOKKE
BRUSSELS
1335 hrs
MANNHEIM
Danube
Mosel
LUDWIGSHAFEN
HEIDELBERG
BELGIUM
1405
TRIER
STUTTGART
MUNICH
LUX.
LUXEMBOURG
SAARBRUCKEN
KARLSRUHE
ARRAS
Rhine
1550 hrs
METZ
RHEIMS
FRANCE
SWITZ.
AUSTRIA

The 14 troop carrier groups which launched the airborne invasion of France, 6th June 1944

434th	Troop Carrier Group	Aldermaston, England
435th	Troop Carrier Group	Welford, England
436th	Troop Carrier Group	Membury, England
437th	Troop Carrier Group	Ramsbury, England
438th	Troop Carrier Group	Greenham Common, England
439th	Troop Carrier Group	Upotlery, England
440th	Troop Carrier Group	Exeter, England
441st	Troop Carrier Group	Merryfield, England
442nd	Troop Carrier Group	Weston Zoyland, England
313th	Troop Carrier Group	Folkingham, England
314th	Troop Carrier Group	Saltby, England
315th	Troop Carrier Group	Stanhoe, England
61st	Troop Carrier Group	Barkston, England
316th	Troop Carrier Group	Cottesmore, England

weakened the enemy. On 27 July the Germans began to retreat on the left, and over the next ten days the US 1st Army pushed rapidly through Brittany and Normandy.

Now the Allies had their breakthrough, thanks to the continuous and accurate air bombardment of the greatest strategic and tactical air forces of all time, the 8th and 9th Air Forces. From 26–31 July the assault continued and armored columns advanced practically nonstop to Marigny, Canisy and Periers. Coutances fell on 28 July and Avranches on 31 July. The USAAF was called on continuously to provide a different kind of service, close-in ground support. The 1 August saw the arrival of the US 3rd Army, commanded by one of the greatest tank commanders of all times, Lt General George S Patton Jr. Patton's 3rd Army, together with Lt General Courtney H Hodges' 1st Army, came under the 15th Army Group of Lt General Omar N Bradley. Immediately, Patton spearheaded his columns south to isolate the Brittany peninsula and the ports of Brest, Lorient and St Nazaire. To support adequately Patton's 3rd Army, the 19th TAC was created, under the command of Major General Otto P Weyland, who was to have great difficulties with Patton, as the 3rd Army advanced at breakneck speed.

Patton sent one corps to mop up in Brittany and then turned east, forgot about his flanks with Weyland's guarantee to keep the Germans south of the Loire off his back, and drove like 'a bat out of hell' for Paris. In two weeks, he reached Paris, in two more he was less than 60 miles from Germany. The point remains that if Weyland had not been able to knock out the bridges over the Loire and keep the Germans from crossing, and cover Patton's mad tankers, then Patton might not have reached Paris in two weeks. The whole advance was one of close air and ground coordination. The fall of Paris and the triumphant Allied entry into the city was the culmination of a long and hard advance.

Opposite: *B-26 over the Weser knocks out a bridge.*
Above: *Damage inflicted on a B-17 of the 493rd Bomb Group.*

Below: *B-17 of the 8th AF over the recently-bombed Tempelhof Field.*

Above: *A bombed-out repair shop and hangar at the Dornier aircraft factory at Oberpfaffenhofen, Bavaria.*
Above right: *This was Hitler's Chancellery after the air raids.*
Above far right: *P-51s give cover to a closely knit formation of B-24s.*
Right: *The devastated walled city of Nuremberg.*

The period from 15 August to 5 September was one of the most dramatic in the European war. In three weeks, two enemy countries retired from the war, and another tried. Eisenhower continued advancing from Falaise to Brussels, Namur and Verdun, freeing more European cities and destroying eight German divisions.

Meanwhile, Operation Dragoon, the the invasion of southern France was going full strength, the US 7th Army and French 1st Army had landed on 15 August and by 3 September had taken Lyons. The coastal defenses were strong, but there was practically no air opposition – not surprising really as the odds pitted 2000 Allied aircraft against a paltry 200 the Germans scraped together.

The initial invasion was launched when the 50th and 53rd Troop Carrier Wings participated in troop drops, along with over 330 A-20s and B-26s which bombed Marseille and Fort de Chantilly ammunition and fuel dumps, rail bridges, and the coastal defenses at St Malo. Air cover was provided for five infantry and armored divisions. The 12th Air Force units bombed Istres, Le-Vallon and Rhone Valley targets while the US 7th Army attempted to isolate Dragoon beaches. The US Special Forces attacked Levant and Port Cros Islands and secured the left flank. The 1st Airborne Task Force dropped in the rear of the assault beaches and secured the invasion sectors from the interior. The French Naval Assault Group landed southwest of Cannes and secured the right flank, while the French commanders cleared coastal defenses. The US 6th Corps landed three divisions at 0800 hours, 15 August, between Nice and Toulon. The 12th Air Force was kept busy throughout the day, supporting the invasion, hitting beaches, enemy troop concentrations and gun positions. This continuous massive air support went on as the US 6th Corps pushed forward and overran the Gestapo HQ near Châteauroux on 17 August. The advance quickened and by 2 September the Allies had taken 50,000 prisoners. Lyons fell on 3 September and by 11 September the Allies were approaching Dijon. By that time, the US 3rd Army was not far away and on 15 September Eisenhower took control of the southern armies, which were amalgamated into 6th Army Group under General Devers.

The battle of Normandy was a success and had cost the enemy 200,000 men killed, wounded or missing; he had lost 600 tanks, numerous guns and other irreplaceable equipment. But the victory would not have been possible without complete air superiority during the invasion.

The Second Quebec Conference (Octagon Conference) was held in September 1944. Its primary concern was to define the relationship between the war against Germany and the war against Japan. While the conference was in progress, the Allied Command was preparing the final phase of the campaign in Europe. On 9 September Eisenhower told the Combined Chiefs of Staff that he intended to destroy the German Armed Forces and occupy the heart of Germany, and that he pro-

posed to attack the heavily defended Ruhr and Saar areas. The key to victory would first be to break the Siegfried Line and seize bridges across the Rhine. The central force would take Brest, breakthrough the Siegfried Line where it covered the Saar and take Frankfurt. The northern force would capture Antwerp, break the Siegfried Line near the Ruhr and seize it. The 1st Allied Airborne Army, commanded by Lt General Lewis Brereton, would support the operations across the Rhine.

On 10 September General Montgomery proposed that the attack should be carried out on Grave, Nijmegen and Arnhem, with 'A' priority over all operations. This was Operation Market Garden and it was destined to failure. The 1st Allied Airborne Army was to be dropped behind the enemy lines at Nijmegen and the British airborne at Arnhem on 17 September. The American units captured Nijmegen but the British were practically wiped out in heavy fighting at Arnhem. This ended the advance north and east, and the attempt to flank the Siegfried Line. The autumn of 1944 saw the Allies building up supplies for the next advance.

Through September and October, the Allies advanced steadily and the Allied Air Forces were in the forefront of the fighting.

The next move occurred in the very early hours of 16 December 1944, when eight Panzer divisions and ten infantry divisions supported by over 500 tanks, 300 assault guns, 1300 pieces of heavy artillery and 1350 aircraft of Luftwaffe West were launched in a final blitzkrieg in what became known as the Ardennes Counteroffensive – The Battle of the Bulge. This force was commanded by Field Marshal Gerd von Rundstedt. The Germans broke through the US 1st Army's lines almost immediately. The enemy then dropped special paratroopers behind the Allied lines to disrupt communications and if possible stop reinforcements from arriving. Von Rundstedt picked the right time for his offensive. The weather was extremely bad, cloud and fog aided the German advance immeasurably. The

Above: *A bombed-out submarine shipyard in Bremen after the raid of 14 March 1945.*
Above right: *The Munich City Hall was built by Kaiser Wilhelm in 1910. After the war it housed the Allied Military Government.*

Below: *An Me-109 was grounded by the 8th Air Force in Augsburg. The Messerschmitt factory is camouflaged by trees in the background.*

19th TAC

100th Fighter Wing
354th Fighter Group
362nd Fighter Group
363rd Fighter Group
371st Fighter Group
303rd Fighter Wing
36th Fighter Group
358th Fighter Group
373rd Fighter Group
405th Fighter Group
406th Fighter Group

29th TAC

366th Fighter Group
370th Fighter Group
373rd Fighter Group
405th Fighter Group
406th Fighter Group

Above: *A B-17 is destroyed in the air on 8 April 1945.*

supporting US air units were grounded most of the time. The Luftwaffe flew over 150 ground sorties in support of the main column. For the first time, the Allies did not have complete control of the air.

The 9th Bombardment Division (formerly 9th Bomber Command), managed to get airborne on 18 December and dropped 274 tons in support of besieged US troops. But the adverse weather limited the US air sorties to a bare minimum. The 5th Panzer Army had passed Malmédy and was pushing toward Stavelot, the 6th Panzer Army had reached St Vith, and in the south Wiltz fell and the Germans were pushing towards the key crossroads of Bastogne.

Below: *Men of the 381st Bomb Group celebrate V-E Day in their NCO Club.*

Intelligence was lacking on the dispersal of the German advance and volunteers were asked to fly on photo missions. Captain Richard Cassidy and 2nd Lt Abe Jaffe, 67th Tactical Reconnaissance Group took off in response to the request. Passing Stavelot, they sighted over 60 Panzer tanks and a column pushing through the fog. Cassidy radioed his report to 9th TAC and the 365th and 368th Fighter Groups scrambled immediately to intercept the Panzer column. The 365th 'Hell Hawks' and 368th 'Panzer Dusters', commanded by Colonel Ray Stecker and Lt Colonel Frank Perego respectively, found the Panzer force and managed to seriously damage over 32 armored vehicles. By 1700 hours the crack Adolf Hitler Division was halted in its tracks.

The 21 December saw the Germans attempting to widen the gap. They had completely surrounded the 101st Airborne Division at the key town of Bastogne. The Germans asked the American commander to surrender and it took a while for the negative reply to sink in. Although the Germans advanced they could not widen the gap to push through additional troops and armor. US air units were now being used constantly for interdiction, close-in ground support and bombing missions against railroad yards, supply depots, armored columns and strategic bridges. The air operations between 23–27 December formed the key to the containment of the German counter-offensive. By 26 December Patton's 3rd Army had broken through to relieve the 101st at Bastogne. Elements of the 9th, 19th and 29th TACs had saved the day illustrating once again the distinct advantage of air power in modern warfare. Air power had destroyed German communications, eliminated their air support units and bombed their advance columns into oblivion. The month of January 1945 saw the Allies mop up after the Bulge and prepare for the coming advance on the Rhine.

During the months directly preceding the Bulge and afterwards, the USSTAF and Bomber Command policy had been to hit two primary targets: transport and oil. The effect of this steady bombardment had its results. Speer, Hitler's industrial genius, believed that bad weather and an ineffective Allied bombing policy was what could save future German production. But now weather mattered less with improved artificial aids and bombing was becoming more and more accurate. The attack on oil truly worried Speer; he predicted, 'complete disaster and catastrophe.' His measures could no longer avert the final collapse.

On 10 January 1945 the 8th dispatched over 912 heavies to attack bridges, marshaling yards, five airfields and various targets of opportunity. The bombers were escorted by three fighter groups. Another P-51 group attacked the marshaling yards at Neustadt. Results were excellent but twenty bombers were lost to AA fire. Over 30 B-26s were sent to take out road bridges and communications centers but aborted due to adverse weather conditions. The 19th TAC flew escort for medium bombers of the 9th Air Force, attacked bridges, and supported the US 3rd, 7th, 12th and 20th Corps around the Saint Hubert-Bastogne-Wiltz sectors. The 10 January was a typical day according to a US 19th TAC pilot from Connecticut. Another pilot, who was wounded on 16 January

Opposite: *These B-24s participated in the daylight raid over Berlin on 18 March 1945.*

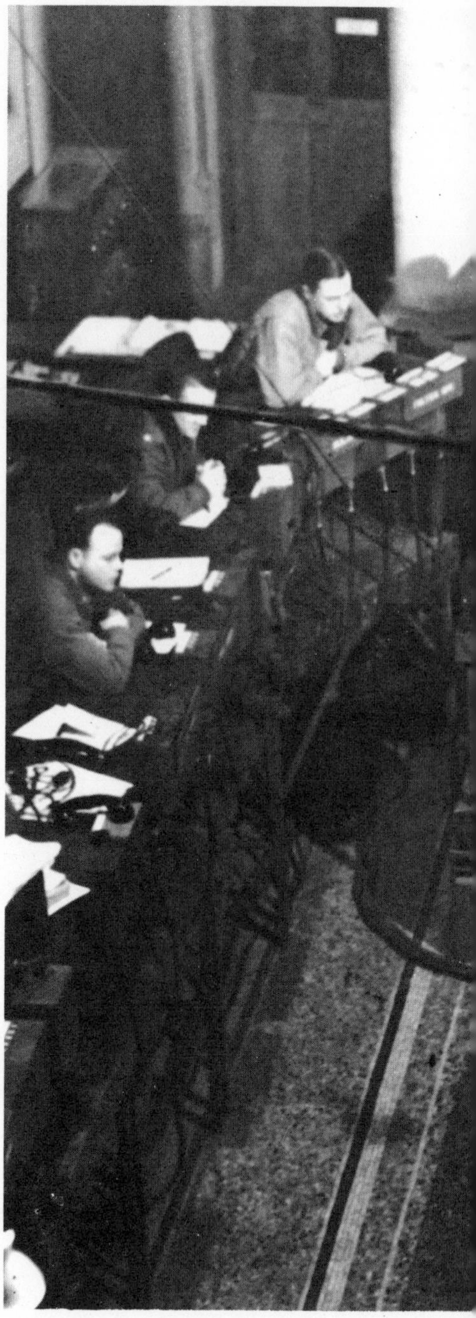

Top left: *Lt William B King leans on the wing of the* Georgia Peach *chalks up another victory. In 44 missions he has knocked out two Messerschmitts, a locomotive and two German ammunition carriers.*
Above left: *Radar operator of a B-29 Superfortress.*
Left: *B-17s en route to Germany.*

near Houffalize, always thought himself a connoisseur of fine wines. He got his chance when he bailed out near a wine cellar. This lieutenant said he never tasted wine so exquisite in all of his twenty years.

Two groups which earned fame during the early months of 1945 were the 405th and 406th Fighter Group, 9th Air Force. The 405th was primarily engaged in providing air support for ground forces until 8 May 1945. It bombed bays, roads, supply depots and troops during the Battle of the Bulge, and hit Luftwaffe airfields

Above: *Fighter Control Center of a TAC headquarters.*
Right: *Berchtesgaden, the Eagle's Nest of the Führer, came under Allied attack in the last days of the war.*

and marshaling yards when the Allies crossed the Rhine in March. The 406th flew interdictory missions during the drive to the Moselle-Saar sector. It transferred operations to the Ardennes and flew close-in air support sorties for the Bastogne garrison. It received a record Distinguished Unit Citation (DUC) for operating exclusively within a ten mile radius of Bastogne from 23–27 March 1944. It flew strikes against the Rhine troops, enemy troops and artillery positions through the first months of 1945. It was units like the 405th and 406th Fighter Groups which gave the USAAF something to be proud of – *esprit de corps* and a feeling of togetherness.

One of the many units who witnessed the successful conclusion of the war was the 20th Fighter Group, 8th Air Force. Its history goes as far back as 18 October 1927, when it was known as the 20th Balloon Group. It moved to Kings Cliffe, England, 26 August 1943 to become an integral part of 8th Fighter Command. Under Colonel Barton M Russell, the 20th flew its first combat sortie with P-38s in late December 1943. It was engaged in escort duty for medium and heavy bombers, but strafed secondary targets whenever in a good tactical position. In March 1944 the 20th flew its initial fighter-bomber mission and also dive-bombed airfields, armored vehicles, trains, tugs, bridges, gun emplacements, barracks and communications centers throughout Belgium, France and Germany. Its most successful targets were locomotives, thus its nickname the 'Loco Group'. They took an active part in the Normandy invasion in June 1944. The group

received new P-51s in July 1944 to replace the older P-38s. The 20th participated in the Allied attack on Holland in September 1944. They flew escort for bombers attacking Germany and attacked rail lines, trains, armored vehicles, power stations and troop concentrations along the Siegfried Line. They played an active role in the Battle of the Bulge by escorting medium and heavy bombers to the front. The group carried out fighter-bomber missions till the end of the war. One of its ex-commanders was to become world famous as commander, 8th Air Force, Lt General Ira C Eaker. The 20th earned its motto: 'Victory by Valor.'

The 4 February 1945 brought together the Big Three – Roosevelt, Stalin and Churchill – at Yalta in the

Above: *Glenn Miller's Army Air Force Band was the 'voice' of the Air Force during the war.*
Below: *The nose of this B-17 was shot away by enemy flak over Cologne, but it made its way back to England safely.*

Crimea for a conference. Also Eden, Hopkins, Molotov and Stettinius were in attendance. Matters discussed were the USSR's entry into war with Japan, policy toward Germany, policy toward a liberated Europe, the Polish problem, the Security Council voting formula and the calling of a United Nations Conference.

The remainder of February saw the 8th and 9th Air Force hit targets at Vianden, Nüremberg, Echternach, Lützkendorf, Kempen and Leipzig. The 12th and 15th Air Forces struck objectives at Graz, the Brenner Pass and Zagreb. The Allies continued their push through the Rhine. On 22 March 1945 they began their assault across the river and by 1 April the Ruhr was surrounded. On 25 April the US and Russian Forces met at the Elbe River

Above: *Major Glenn Miller gave up his fabulous career as a bandleader when he joined the 8th. He subsequently gave his life in December 1944 in a still unresolved air crash over the Channel.*

Above: Ferocious Frankie, *Col Wallace Hopkins' P-51, drops two 500lb bombs over France.*
Below: *This B-17 crashed over Berlin minutes later. No parachutes were seen to open.*

Above: *Bob Hope gets his signs straight from Capt Billy Southworth of baseball's Boston Braves.*

Above: *Major James Stewart of film fame receives the Air Medal after 10 missions over Germany.*

Above: *Staff Sgt Quinlan of Yonkers, NY, tail-gunner of the* Memphis Belle.
Below: *A convoy flight of B-26s on their way from the States to England.*

and the strategic bombing operations were halted and operations were planned for dropping foodstuffs, medicine and other essentials to the needy.

The German Army was defeated; the P-51s and B-17s flew at will practically unchallenged. April ended with Hitler's death. Actually, it was extremely lucky for him because one GI from Sulfur Springs, Texas had a warrant to arrest one Adolf Hitler for murder and to bring him back to Texas for trial. In High Wycombe, former HQ 8th Air Force, now 8th Fighter Command HQ, a grandmother had her one ambition come true when she rode a US Army jeep through the center of town to celebrate VE-Day.

The 7th May 1945 witnessed the cessation of hostilities in the European Theater of Operations. By mid-June US air units which were not programmed for garrison duty or redeployment were sent home. After three years of fighting the boys were going home.

Years of strategic bombing had been decisive in the defeat of Hitler's Nazi Germany. What strategic bombing at its height could achieve was proved in early 1945. In the beginning Roosevelt and Churchill knew that when the United States entered the war, the only way America could immediately help its Allies was by sending supplies and convoying them across the Atlantic. This phase was handled by the United States Navy. The only other way aid could be sent was to dispatch an air force. The 8th Air Force had been deployed to England in early May 1942. By 1945 it accomplished its task – the defeat of Hitler and the freedom of Western Europe.

Below: *Flying Tigers leap into action as they run for their P-40s. The Flying Tigers were incorporated into the 14th Air Force after Pearl Harbor Day.*

Over the Hump

The China–Burma–India Theater (CBI) was an integral part of the Pacific War. It is extremely ironic that although the military objectives were successful, the political aspects were such a total failure.

The United States was unable to aid its ally Great Britain in retaining her Asiatic Empire. The Pearl Harbor debacle, fall of the Philippines and Japanese advance throughout Southeast Asia placed the CBI theater at the bottom of the priority list. With the immediate fall of Burma and the remainder of southeast Asia, the Nationalist Chinese under Generalissimo Chiang Kai-shek were beleaguered in Chungking. The US through continuous air operations which flew supplies and equipment to Chiang Kai-shek over the Hump, definitely kept China in the war, and tied up a tremendous number of Japanese forces which could have been utilized advantageously in some other Pacific sector.

The Allied Chief in Chungking was General Joseph (Vinegar Joe) Stilwell whose active dislike for Chiang Kai-shek (Peanut) was well-known and mutual. Stilwell was the US's expert on Chinese affairs. His first tour was in 1911 and he spent most of his active career in China. Stilwell, a man of character and integrity, could not stand the crooked dealing of the Generalissimo but Roosevelt knew that throw-

Right: *Lt Francis J Cahill, Intelligence Officer of the 40th Bomb Group in the CBI Theater, keeps his men abreast of events in the Philippines outside his sphere of operations.*
Far right: *Armorers of the 14th Air Force in China give a Chinese guard a glance at their copy of* Yank, *a GI magazine published during the war.*
Below: *An al fresco Christmas dinner somewhere in China in 1942.*

12

Left: *Eyes aloft for idealistic pilots of the US Air Force, stationed in the CBI theater.*

ing Chiang to the wolves would only prolong the conflict.

The CBI not only had the physical problems of living in the east to endure but also did not have a defined goal, something to fight for. The average American airman in China, without his usual can of beer and PX rations for which Air Transport Command (ATC) allocation could not be spared, disgusted and unused to such absolute squalor and filth, alienated by the callous cruelties of Chinese life, and with no understanding of the deprivations and hunger for the 'horn of plenty' that led Chinese graft and thievery to flourish unchecked, did not, as the idealists like to believe, learn

and understand through contact that all men are brothers. In fact, these airmen came to regard all Chinese as sneaky, inefficient, unreliable, corrupt and hopeless. In turn, the Chinese thought the American airmen of the 14th Air Force stupid, coarse, contemptible, brutal barbarians. As the kudos and promotions went elsewhere, ridden by scandals, frustrations and animosities, the CBI was an unrewarding and unhappy theater.

The man that Chiang Kai-shek chose to build his new air force was a rather remarkable fighter pilot, Colonel Claire Chennault, who was retired from the US Air Corps because of deafness and internal disagreement with higher authority.

Chennault and T V Soong were sent to Washington to put China's needs across the table. Chennault was

Above: *Wingate briefs 1st Air Commando Force pilots on invasion plans.*
Below: *Evacuees from Burma unload belongings at Ohabua, India in 1943.*

an old fighter pilot, a fanatic when it came to pursuit aircraft. He had originally started out as a high school teacher, in Texas, went on to officer training in 1917 and was commissioned into the Infantry Reserve. He transferred to the Aviation Section of the Signal Corps later on because of his avid interest in aviation. He stayed with the new Air Corps during the 1920s and experimented in air pursuit and tactics; in fact, he wrote a textbook called *The Role of Defensive Pursuit.* He was a proponent of fighter aircraft and the importance of fighter escorts. However, the Air Corps had adopted the Douhet theory that successive waves of bombers would be self-protecting. It was not until the Schweinfurt raids of 1943 that his theories on fighter escorts were totally appreciated. He was not popular with the Air Corps but he was highly recommended to Chiang. By 1938 Colonel Chennault of the Chinese Air Force had successfully begun a major airfield construction program and was the force behind the American Volunteer Group (AVG), better known to the world as 'The Flying Tigers'.

In October 1940 the Chinese government requested that the United States send an air force of 500 aircraft manned by American pilots who would fly in defense of China. Chiang stated the need was urgent and he had the cheek to offer a large return. He believed emphatically that American planes and pilots could eliminate the Japanese Naval threat at their own bases. Chiang, an ardent supporter of air power, was voicing the thoughts of one of the most controversial future air force commanders of the war, his present advisor, Colonel Claire Chennault.

Left: *Endless rows of Jeeps and other vehicles line up in Victoria Park, Calcutta, to be shipped to China and Burma.* Below: *Chinese workmen roll the runway on a recently constructed US air base in south-western China.*

Discussions were carried out despite the extreme caution urged by Secretary of War Henry L Stimson who thought the whole scheme was rather half-cocked. General George C Marshall, Army Chief of Staff, declared the entire program 'impractical'. The force which was eventually put together consisted of 100 P-40 fighters. Even this small force had to be taken from a consignment scheduled for Great Britain.

Pearl Harbor forced the United States to depart from its sympathetic role in the Sino-Japanese conflict. The United States saw China as an obstacle to Japanese expansion and decided to aid China in her struggle. Aid was first given to China by the Roosevelt regime in March 1941 in the form of monetary loans which were immediately followed by Lend-Lease aid in May 1941. Chiang requested an air mission be sent to China soon afterwards, and the mission was headed by General H B Claggett, commander of the Philippine Air Force. The Claggett report emphasized the urgent need for fighters to protect Chinese cities and bombers to strike against Japanese military facilities. It was suggested that 350 aircraft be sent to China manned by US pilots. This military report was direct corroboration of Chennault's scheme for the creation of the American Volunteer Group.

Recruitment of pilots had to be conducted with secrecy because some states were still neutral. All transactions were made through a private corporation, the Central Aircraft Manufacturing Company (CAMCO), and Chinese Defense Supplies. AVG recruiters were considered employees of CAMCO. Therefore, all those

who volunteered to serve in China were also CAMCO employees and Chennault's title was CAMCO supervisor. So the whole thing was an elaborate scheme to minimize official US involvement.

By June 1941 the 100 pilots and 150 technicians were recruited right on schedule. The volunteers met in San Francisco in July, and after a short orientation briefing boarded the Dutch liner *Jaegersfontaine* bound for Malaya. Upon reaching the Hawaiian Islands, the liner rendezvoused with two US naval vessels and was escorted past Japanese-held islands to Manila. Then it proceeded to Singapore, where a transfer was accomplished to a Norwegian freighter bound for Rangoon. This initial contingent arrived on 28 July 1941, followed by a second in September.

Originally, Chennault had planned that Kunming, China would be headquarters for the AVG. But the Chinese were unable to complete preparations prior to the monsoon season. Instead the AVG advance element was sent to Kyedow airfield, near Toungoo in Burma. Kyedow's only claim to fame was its 4000ft asphalt runway. It was constructed and operated by the British Colonial Government in Burma and only leased to the Chinese for training purposes. The real reason for this was the delicate international situation. Great Britain could not offer to have Kyedow used as an attack installation against Japanese forces. Kyedow definitely made a lasting impression upon the AVG; in most cases, it was their first time overseas and the hot, humid and uncomfortable climate left a lasting mark.

The AVGs arrival was a bit late for deterrence but just in time to fight. This group of men consisted of US Army and Naval pilots who were attracted by salaries of $750 a month, plus $500 for every Japanese aircraft destroyed. Technicians were paid between $150–350 per month, plus bonuses.

The Burma Campaign began on 10 December 1941, when 21 aircraft of an AVG squadron reinforced the RAF unit at Rangoon. It was a vital necessity for Chiang to commit Chennault's virgin force to the defense of Burma. The Burma Road was China's only link with the outside world and it was imperative that this lifeline be kept open.

The Japanese attacked Rangoon on 23 December expecting negative resistance. In the engagement, ten Japanese aircraft had been destroyed, but the defenders had lost four AVG and five RAF fighters, a major disaster. Even worse was the results of the fire bombing of the city; thousands of civilians were killed and wounded.

Right: *Part of the crew of the B-24* The Goon *in China.*
Below: *Lord Louis Mountbatten speaks to men of the 1st Air Commando Unit in India under his command. Mountbatten was loathed by his American counterpart in China, 'Vinegar Joe' Stilwell.*

Below: *Control tower of Myitkyina North Airfield, Burma, constructed by the 1888th Engineer Aviation Battalion of the 10th Air Force.*

Above: *Major General Claire Chennault, Commander of the 14th Air Force in China.*

This type of attack continued through the end of December with the AVG wreaking havoc on the Japanese aircraft using the tactics taught by Chennault. The stark reality was that each time a P-40 was destroyed or damaged it was virtually impossible to replace. The Japanese only had to whittle the AVG down and every attack was doing just that.

Meanwhile, the Japanese were forging ahead on the ground, steadily advancing on Rangoon. On 23 February 1942 the Battle of the Sittang Bridge saw the Japanese defeat the Indian brigades and advance past Pegu. Now the threat to Rangoon was ominous. By 6 March 1942 all Allied Forces, equipment and supplies were withdrawn or destroyed as the Japanese entered the city.

After the fall of Rangoon, the Japanese Army advanced north, along the Irrawaddy and Sittang rivers, toward the Allied airfields near Toungoo. The AVG and RAF fought a holding action from their base at Magwe, but the Japanese retaliated with massive bombing missions to reduce Magwe. The base was abandoned, the AVG retreating to China, the RAF to India.

The Japanese advance continued practically unchecked as Kyedow, Prome, Toungoo, Meiktila, Yemangyaung, Mandalay and Lashio fell one by one. Lashio was a critical blow to the Chinese, as it was the southern terminus of the Burma Road; they would never have recovered had it not been for the 'Hump'.

The AVG record in the Burma campaign was exceptional with 299 Japanese aircraft destroyed and over 300 damaged. Considering what they had to work with and the conditions, the AVG record was impressive.

At the same time, the newly formed 10th Air Force was fighting to establish itself in India and plans for the Hump were being finalized. The Allied Combined Chiefs of Staff realized that supplies would have to reach China by air, so transport aircraft were dispatched to the CBI theater. The problem of transports was a sore spot for General Arnold; the USAAF only had 216 transports available for the planned war effort. The China airlift operation was given third priority and received 139 transports.

MYITKYINA
NORTH AIRFIELD
CONS. BY 1888 INGR AVN BN
10TH U.S. ARMY AIR FORCE

The actual Hump flight only lasted a few hours. It would start when a C-47 pilot and his crew took off from Dingan and flew east out of the Brahmaputra Valley. The first obstacle was the 10,000ft Patkai Mountain Range, then the 14,000ft Kumon Mountains. Next was a series of 14,500–16,000ft ridges separated by the Irrawaddy, Mekong and Salween rivers, the prelude to the 20,000ft Lantung Ranges. That was 'the Hump' but it was not just the mountains that made it difficult; it also involved flying through the worst weather in the world.

The weather at least provided cloud cover and gave the India–China Wing aircraft some protection from the roaming Japanese fighter. Pilots had to fly their transports at 20,000ft to avoid icing and extreme turbulence. In fact, the majority of flights between Dingan and Kunming were made on instruments; the crew very seldom saw the ground.

Claire L Chennault and the exploits of his famed 'Flying Tigers' are well-known. But less well-known is his nickname, 'Old Leatherface', coined by his men because of the severe wind-burns he received in the open cockpit flying of the 1920s and 1930s.

The AVG as an independent entity could only hope for supplies and equipment from the United States. But after Pearl Harbor, there was absolutely no reason to stay independent of the United States' China–Burma–India command. Besides as a component part of the USAAF, Chennault could expect a higher priority for equipment, supplies and personnel. Lt General Joseph Stilwell, Commander in Chief, China–Burma–India Command, presented Chennault with the proposed merger in March 1942. Stilwell was very surprised at Chennault's acceptance because he believed the AVG commander would not want to merge with the 10th Air Force. In April 1942, the AVG was officially incorporated with the 10th Air Force. Chennault was reactivated by the US Army and promoted to Brigadier General, and assumed command of the new China Air Task Force (CATF), the forerunner of the 14th Air Force.

The CATF was not officially activated until 4 July 1942 because of the reluctance of the majority of the AVG to accept induction into the USAAF. The reason for this was most of the men had originally joined the AVG to get away from the official army red tape, rules and regimentation. Finally, new men and equipment arrived and the CATF became a fact. With the new name came two B-25 squadrons and one B-24 group, the 308th Bombardment Group (H).

There were difficulties from the beginning. HQ 10th Air Force was in Delhi, India, 2200 miles away from Chennault's Kunming HQ which resulted in serious communication problems and lack of coordination. The most important problem was the mutual dislike shared by Brigadier General Clayton Bissell, 10th Air Force Commander and Chennault. Even Chiang Kai-shek disliked Bissell who he thought acted like an old woman on occasions. Thus Chennault distrusted the two men to whom he was subordinate, Bissell and Stilwell, and they disliked his independence and arrogance which bordered on insubordination. But they were at a disadvantage because of Chennault's close personal friendship with the Generalissimo and Madame Chiang.

The missions of the China Air Task Force were to defend the eastern and southern approaches to the Hump, to attack Japanese shipping and supply routes, and to provide air support for Chinese ground forces. Early 1943 saw the supply problem worsen for Chennault's CATF to the point where offensive missions were canceled due to fuel shortages. Chennault, vehement as ever, blamed this on Bissell and Stilwell and recommended the immediate separation of the CATF from the 10th Air Force. He wanted an air force in China independent of Bissell's Delhi command.

In October 1942 Wendell Willkie, the unsuccessful presidential candidate in 1940, was sent to China as President Roosevelt's special emissary. Chennault had private talks with Willkie and succeeded in converting him to his way of thinking. Willkie returned to Washington with a letter from Chennault to Roosevelt. This letter stated Chennault's belief that

Below: *Chennault says goodbye to diva Lily Pons and conductor André Kostelanetz in China in 1945.*

Japan could be defeated by air power alone.

Roosevelt read his letter with enthusiasm and passed it on to the Joint Chiefs. The Joint Chiefs, especially Generals Marshall and Arnold, reacted very coolly to this proposed scheme; his plan was considered unrealistic because of the logistical problems involved. Although the Joint Chiefs were against giving Chennault an independent command, Roosevelt eventually capitulated in the face of pressure from the China Lobby in Congress and his own political associates.

Controversy and politics surrounded Chennault's command in the CBI. He had his admirers and followers, but he was an unconventional officer in a conventional service. His weakness was in logistics and that was what the CBI was all about – supplies, equipment and replacements. General Hap Arnold considered him a black sheep.

On 8 March 1943 Roosevelt ordered a separate air force for Chennault, independent of the 10th Air Force, but not of Stilwell. 'Vinegar Joe' and 'Old Leatherface' were not on the best of terms due to Chiang's obvious preference for the air-force commander over his superior. Roosevelt overlooked Arnold's lack of enthusiasm for Chennault and also overruled the War Department's *quid pro quo* approach to China. Roosevelt's only military mistakes occurred when he did not take the advice of his military staff. This was one such error; the creation of the 14th Air Force was unrealistic because the logistic requirements for its support did not exist and because of this Chennault could not achieve air superiority over China in six months as he had predicted.

Chennault was fighter-oriented being a pursuit man of the old Air Corps school. Therefore, bombers, especially heavy bombers which ate up valuable gas supplies were not exactly his cup of tea. But they were a necessary part and at the close of the war his 308th Bombardment Group had the most accurate bombing results of the entire United States Army Air Force. This group also had the highest losses and casualties in the 14th Air Force.

Chennault utilized B-24 Liberators because they could also act as their own transports over the Hump. The 308th had to self-support to survive. The Hump was only one segment of the 14th Air Force's 15,000 mile supply-line that started with a 12,000 mile sea lane from the United States to Karachi, India. But the toughest part came next, the 1500 mile railway system across India to Air Transport Command (ATC) airfields south of the Hump. This bypassed what Chennault called 'the critical bottleneck'. Once on the other side of the Hump, fuel and spares for his air force had to be carted by river and road hundreds of miles beyond Kunming which took

Below: *General Lewis Pick after the first convoy passed over the Stilwell Road.*

eight weeks if the conditions were right – a practically non-existent occurrence. The Air Transport Command used one gallon of fuel for each gallon it brought into China. The losses over the route were very heavy indeed; in 36 months of continuous operations the ATC lost 468 aircraft.

The 14th Air Force was under an extreme disadvantage. Roosevelt had promised Chennault a minimum of 4700 tons of supplies for July and August 1943. The actual total carried over the Hump was 200 tons less than the quote. Also if Chennault had checked the cargo manifest, he would have noticed that over 50 percent of these supplies were allocated to Chiang's men. Therefore, his portion was just barely enough for survival. Finally, by September, the tonnage increased to 10,000 tons but the 14th received less than 7200 tons.

Chennault's critics were quick to jump on this saying that airlift was not up to the task of transporting large quantities of matériel to sustain the offensive and Chiang's Nationalist Army as well. He was now paying the price for overconfidence. The airlift failure was not caused by a lack of aircraft but by the bottlenecks between Calcutta and Assam. Supplies enroute from Calcutta to airfields in Assam were moved slowly and sometimes unsuccessfully because the railroads between Bengal and Assam were inadequate and outdated for this type of massive constant supply movement.

But even worse than the inadequate railroads was the British failure to complete the Assam airfields on time as agreed in the Trident Conference. The Trident Conference was the first strategic meeting to which commanders from the CBI were invited. The European issue was the principal concern, but Chennault, Stilwell and Wavell were the centers of interest. The British were in favor of a limited campaign in northern Burma, with the objective of establishing a road from Ledo to Assam, the ultimate objective being Rangoon. This plan was codenamed Anakim. The United States wanted to lift the siege of China, but the British only wanted to re-establish themselves in Burma, especially Singapore. But Roosevelt was swayed in favor of the Chennault–Chiang strategy. Eight airfields were to be operational in Assam, five by June 1943 and the remainder by October 1943. Only two were completed by June as planned.

Nonetheless, the 14th Air Force under Chennault's direction changed from a guerrilla outfit to a fully operational air force despite delays and setbacks in receiving valuable supplies. The 14th was the smallest army air force in World War II, but it was responsible for the largest land area – Burma, all of China, the Formosan straights, Indo-China and Thailand. It is a matter of note that by the end of the war, the 14th's 308th Bombardment Group's B-24 Liberators, had the best bombing record of the entire USAAF, quite an achievement for a lone bombardment group in the backwaters of Asia.

On 4 May 1943, the 308th having built up its supply reserves finally undertook its primary mission. Eighteen unescorted B-24s struck the airfield, oil refinery and fuel storage area at Samah Bay, on the southern portion of Hainan Island, in the heaviest bombing mission in China to that date. Air opposition was negative, and AA fire was very light and totally inaccurate. The mission was a resounding success and Chennault was quite impressed with the results.

The ever-present supply problem would never allow the massive strategic bombing missions so common in Europe, but Chennault revised traditional bombing tactics to fit each and every situation. Consequently, the 14th Air Force became noted for its low level bombing specialty. He went further and borrowed General George C Kenney's ship-bombing tactics against moving ships. The B-25s would come straight in at mast height and release their bombs to skip across the surface of the water. Evasion or defensive action was impossible.

Meanwhile, directly after the Cairo Conference in November 1943, the first raids on Formosa were successfully conducted. Chennault's 14th destroyed 42 Japanese aircraft on the ground in twelve minutes without a single casualty or damaged aircraft. The results had far-reaching implications though, because now the Japanese were convinced that this thorn in their side had to be destroyed. An immediate air and ground offensive was initiated against east China by the Japanese Command, to neutralize the 14th Air Force. Chinese hopes of stemming the enemy advance depend-

Below: *B-29 Superfortress at a Chinese airfield.*

ed upon the 14th's ability to halt them very quickly. Chennault was not receiving enough supplies, was committed to the Burma campaign and to protect the B-29 bases around Chungking, in addition to supporting the Chinese Army; with his meager force, it was impossible. Stilwell blamed the whole debacle on Chennault who had promised to prevent a Japanese offensive.

However, in June 1944, Vice-President Henry Wallace arrived in China to survey the situation. It was to be the most controversial of the war. Stilwell and Chennault only had 24 hours notice of Wallace's arrival. Stilwell was in Burma and could not return to Chungking, consequently, Wallace spent the majority of his time with Chennault and Chiang. By the time Wallace returned to Washington, he was converted to Chiang's way of thinking. Wallace departed with the firm impression that Stilwell should be relieved immediately and Chennault's supply requests fulfilled. He recommended that General Albert Wedemeyer replace Stilwell. This situation got progressively worse as one faction was pitted against another. The deciding factor was the support of the Joint Chiefs of Staff for Stilwell. Roosevelt could not ignore this and settled the matter by promoting him to full general, a rank only held by Marshall, MacArthur, Eisenhower and Arnold.

Chennault turned his attentions to securing permission for an all-out attack against Hankow. This called for combining his 14th with Major General Curtis LeMay's 20th. Approval was finally received but neither commander could agree upon ordinance or tactics. Chennault wanted to use incendiaries from below 20,000ft and LeMay believed HE would do the trick from above 20,000ft. A compromise was eventually reached between these two 'air warlords', as they really did not want to fight each other. LeMay's heavies would drop incendiaries from above 20,000ft on docks and warehouses. The 14th would hit airfields, the B-25s dropping bombs from low level and B-24s from high altitudes.

On 18 December the raid was launched, and although things did not go as planned the damage estimate was excellent. After the B-29s hit the target, the smoke was so thick the B-25s had to fly on instruments. Chennault's P-40s flew top cover and destroyed 64 Japanese fighters. Not one single US aircraft was lost. The fires caused by the incendiaries burned for three whole days. This was the 14th's largest mission, with more than 200 aircraft over Hankow.

The Hankow mission was the first massive fire-raid conducted by 20th Bomber Command. The result was the decisive factor in LeMay's decision to utilize the low level fire-bombing techniques against the Japanese homeland. For the 308th the war would be over in a few months, the tide had finally ebbed. Chennault's bombers continued to strike, though now at a beaten and ever-retreating enemy.

In the context of the total war, or even of the European Theater and its one thousand bomber raids, the China–Burma–India effort could be considered very minor. But the CBI effort was unique and its men were equal to the task. They fought against overwhelming odds and won.

Chiang Kai-shek's Nationalist Chinese Government held out against the Japanese from 1937–45 which was of immense value to the United States. In the first four years Japanese casualties in China were over 600,000 of which 175,000 were killed, and the Chinese effort cost her $8800 million or two-thirds of her entire military expenditure. From 1941–45 the war cost Japan a further $46,400 million, had 50 percent of the Japanese Army committed, and resulted in a further 396,000 Japanese deaths. To maintain such a large force in China virtually drained Japan of valuable quantities of men, equipment, munitions and supplies which could have been used elsewhere. Therefore, had Chiang made a separate peace, the United States and her Allies would have had to pay a much higher price for the defeat of Japan.

The CBI saw some impressive achievements: the Hump, the pipeline to China, the Ledo Road, the conquest of northern Burma; but the only significant and lasting achievement was the Hump. It was the birthplace and foundation of the massive strategic airlift. Without the Hump, the Berlin Airlift of 1948 would have been impossible. It established techniques for the emergency air movement of troops and equipment, a precedent which was invaluable during the Korean War.

Atomic Offensive

The Japanese were now completely cut off from the South Pacific Theater after the fall of the Philippines; the war economy began a steady decline. Japan now had her back to the wall: her industries were just about at a standstill due to the lack of raw materials; her air force and navy had suffered very heavily and her remaining naval strength was practically immobilized. She *had* to prevent the United States from securing bases in the Bonin and Ryukyu Islands, and Formosa and her garrisons were ordered to fight to the last man. This was the situation that American forces had to fight in the 'Final Assault' on Japan.

In November 1944 the Joint Staff planners had been working on Operation Downfall, the programmed invasion of Japan. The Joint Chiefs of Staff tentatively approved the draft for Operation Olympic, the assault on Kyushu, to begin 1 September 1945, and Operation Coronet, the invasion of Honshu, to begin 1 December 1945. The actual campaigns on Leyte, Luzon, Iwo Jima and Okinawa lasted longer than anticipated, so that Olympic and Coronet had to be postponed, if they were conducted at all.

According to MacArthur's plan, the Kyushu offensive would be preceded by air attacks of great magnitude by aircraft of the Far East Air Force, the 20th Air Force and Pacific Fleet carriers. The air offensive against Japan could not become totally effective until it could be launched from the Mariana Islands, which were captured, primarily for that purpose, in June 1944.

Also in June 1944, the US 20th Air Force's 20th Bomber Command based in India began hitting heavy industrial targets in Manchuria and Japan from its forward airfields near Chengtu, China. The problem here was that the B-29s were at their maximum range and could only strike Kyushu, the southernmost Japanese home island. This was the reason for the offensive in the Marianas, which were only 1200 miles from Tokyo and the all important industrial targets throughout central Japan.

The first airfield was ready at Saipan, in the Marianas, by the end of October 1944. The 73rd Bombardment Wing (Very Heavy) moved to Isley Field, Saipan, in October, followed by the 313th Bombardment Wing (Very Heavy) to North Field, Tinian in December and the 314th Bombardment Wing (Very Heavy) to North Field, Guam in January 1945. In October 1944 General Henry H

Right: *B-24s of 7th AF attack Bonin Islands, Iwo Jima 21 October 1944.*
Below: *Sgt Ellis describes the run over a Japanese ship off the Kuriles.*

Below: *A formation of Consolidated B-24 Liberators roar toward Iwo Jima to obliterate Japanese installations on the Bonin Islands.*

Arnold, ordered the 21st Bomber Command to destroy the Japanese aircraft industry by daylight high-altitude bombing with 500lb HE bombs. The main target area were aircraft factories in and around Tokyo, Yokohama, Kobe, Osaka and Nagoya. On 24 November 1944, 111 B-29s made the first raid on Tokyo since the memorable Doolittle Raid of August 1942. The target area was obscured by clouds and bombing was inaccurate. Although the attacks intensified through December, it was realized that they were in the main highly unsuccessful. The only factory to be damaged during this period was at Kobe.

The setting for the closing stages of the war in the Pacific was determined by the directive of the Joint Chiefs delivered on 30 October 1944, which directed MacArthur, after securing Leyte, to invade Luzon and then support operations by Admiral Nimitz in the Ryukyu Islands in early 1945 to

Above: *An F6F pulls out after chasing a 'Zeke' which crashed into the USS* Suwannee, *25 October 1944.*

provide emergency landing facilities for B-29 bombers and a base for fighter escorts. The invasion of Luzon began in January 1945 and Manila fell by March. Nimitz took Iwo Jima, in the Bonin Islands by the end of March. The next step was Okinawa.

The Ryukyu Islands, of which Okinawa is the largest, lie only 340 miles from Kyushu and Formosa, and 900 miles from Leyte. Okinawa is sixty miles long and five miles wide and is divided in half by the narrow Ishikawa isthmus; south of the isthmus the island is flat with lightly wooded areas and the northern portion is mountainous with thick brush. In the south was the capital Naha, with three airstrips Kadena, Naha and Yontan, and two airfields Machinato and Yonabaru. This was the island which had to be taken in the US advance.

In the preliminary period B-29s of the 21st Bomber Command in the Marianas were diverted from industrial targets in Japan to attack strategic

Above: *The Japanese battleship* Musashi *and the rest of the fleet are attacked from the air in the Battle of the Sibuyan Sea, 24 October 1944.*
Below: *Boeing B-29s prepare to take off for Tokyo at one-minute intervals.*

airfields and targets in Kyushu and to mine the Shimonoseki Strait, the approaches to Hiroshima, Kure and Sasebo.

From January–March 1945 the B-29s continued their daylight precision-bombing raids, but the overall results were very disappointing. It did make the Japanese disperse their aircraft factories and other war-related industries. But the actual damage to them was slight. Major General Curtis LeMay, who assumed command of 21st Bomber Command on 19 January 1945, was in favor of using incendiary bombs against congested Japanese industrial cities which were constructed of wood. This change over from HE to incendiaries was his greatest breakthrough in the war. On 4 February 1945 70 B-29s dropped over 160 tons of incendiaries on Kobe and photo reconnaissance showed that one-tenth of a mile of target area was completely burned out. The results were devastating. The conclusive raid was conducted against Tokyo on 25 February 1945, when 172 B-29s dropped over 450 tons of incendiaries in a daylight raid. The Joint Chiefs considered the record so good as to warrant a change in bombing policy in favor of incendiary attacks against urban industrial areas on a massive scale.

But before this could be put into effect, Nimitz requested 21st Bomber Command on 7 March 1945 to aid in the pre-invasion campaign of Okinawa by hitting Honshu. LeMay decided to continue with the successful incendiary attacks. He realized that for accuracy the bomb clusters would have to be dropped from 5000–10,000ft, and he decided on a night attack as the weather was usually better and the Japanese had few night fighters.

The target was a densely populated area of Tokyo, consisting of over twelve square miles of the most important industrial sections of the city. The 9 March saw 334 B-29s take off and bomb Tokyo with 1700 tons of incendiaries in less than three hours. The result of this raid was that 25 percent of the city was destroyed; casualties were in excess of 185,000; and 267,000 buildings were burned out or gutted. The results were outstanding for only fourteen B-29s destroyed and 42 damaged. Japanese morale was greatly depressed.

The next attack was 11 March against Nagoya, the Japanese aircraft center, by 313 B-29s. An estimated 1800 tons of incendiaries were dropped on target. The results were not as good as in the Tokyo raid because two of the three wings bombed short of the target. One B-29 was lost on take off, and twenty were damaged by AA and fighters.

The third attack was on 13 March by 274 B-29s against Osaka. Despite heavy cloud cover, they managed to drop 1644 tons of incendiary clusters on the industrial heart of the city. Fires spread throughout the city resulting in over eight square miles being burned out. Two B-29s were lost and thirteen damaged. The raid destroyed 135,000 buildings and there were 13,000 casualties.

The fourth raid was the worst. It was conducted on 16 March against Kobe by 307 B-29s. Instead of the normal oil incendiaries, which were out of stock, 2355 tons of combined oil and thermite clusters were dropped. The results were atrocious: 242,000 people made homeless, 2669 killed, 11,289 injured and 65,951 houses destroyed. Three B-29s were lost. The entire eastern section of the business district and the industrial southeast, including the submarine shipyards were totally burned out and gutted.

The last raid was on 20 March against Nagoya again. It was the same except every third aircraft used 500lb HE bombs to disrupt the fire-fighting organizations. Another three square miles were burned out.

The 21st Bomber Command flew 1595 sorties in eleven days and dropped over 9000 tons of incendiary clusters. Four of Japan's key industrial centers were laid to waste and important economic and military targets were destroyed. The Japanese fear of the B-29s was justified. Japan was now helpless against strategic air operations against her major cities.

Above: *Japanese 'Val' dive-bombers prepare to take off from a Japanese aircraft carrier in the South Pacific.*

Below: *B-25s of the Air Apache Group bomb a Japanese destroyer escort.*

Left: *An overview of the bomb damage in Manila, capital of the Philippines on 15 February 1945.*

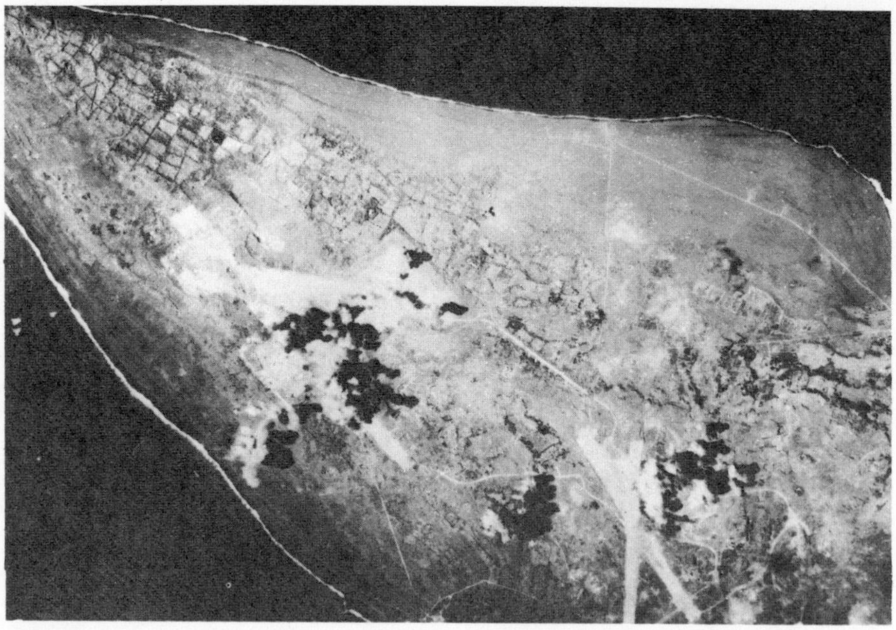

Left: *Japanese airfields and installations in Iwo Jima suffer direct hits from the 7th AAF bombardiers.* Right: *This formation of B-29s was based on Guam in May 1945.*

This was the preview to the Okinawa Campaign. The assault on Okinawa was made on 1 April 1945 but was not an American pushover; heavy losses were sustained between 6–8 April which forced Nimitz once again to call on 21st Bomber Command. This time they were to attack the Kanoya group of airfields in Kyushu. Nimitz also dispatched the fast carrier force north to hit Kyushu. The Japanese retaliated with a massive *Kamikaze* attack on the crowded shipping around Okinawa. Between 19 March–16 April, 41 ships were lost from air attacks alone.

Again Nimitz had to call upon the 21st Bomber Command to hit airfields in Honshu, Kyushu and Shikoku in coordination with 7th Fighter Command on Iwo Jima. From 16 April to 11 May, 75 percent of 21st Bomber Command's effort was diverted from Japan to Okinawa. It flew over 2104 sorties, losing 24 B-29s and sustaining damage to 233, and it claimed 134 enemy fighters destroyed. The 11 May 1945 saw Nimitz release 21st Bomber Command from Okinawa operations as there was now a sufficient force of aircraft on Okinawa. The battle for Okinawa was drawing to a close.

The bloody Okinawa Campaign killed 13,000 Americans, 42,000 civilians and 110,000 Japanese. The aftermath of Okinawa saw relations between MacArthur and Nimitz become very tense. MacArthur's criticism of the campaign was forthright if a bit hard. In one statement, he declared that US casualties on Okinawa were more than all Southwest Pacific Area losses to date, a statement which did not endear him to his naval counterpart.

The US Chiefs of Staff were now preparing for the invasion of Japan which was necessary for her unconditional surrender. The Plan was to blockade the country and initiate an intensive bombing offensive from Okinawa, Iwo Jima and the Marianas to destroy totally enemy communications, industries and morale.

The command structure was changed in the Pacific in April 1945. General MacArthur assumed command of all army ground forces and Admiral Nimitz of all naval forces. General Arnold was still in command of the

Below: *B-29s roll off the main assembly lines and sub-assembly sections on the mezzanine floor of a large factory.*

Above: *The Day Room at Clark Field, Luzon, Philippine Islands, furnishes all types of books, magazines and maps of the different theaters of war. All personnel enjoy the privilege of using this recreational facility.*

20th Air Force in Washington and controlling the strategic bombing offensive against Japan, through the 21st Bomber Command in the Marianas.

With Germany's surrender in May 1945 the United States turned its full attention to finishing the war against Japan. The main courses of action open to the planners were:

(1) to bomb and blockade Japan until she was starved into submission;

(2) to invade Japan;

(3) to frighten Japan through the use of the newly developed atomic bomb;

(4) to change the unconditional surrender terms to allow the Japanese peace party a chance to gain control over the military and overcome opposition to surrender.

The bombing tempo increased against Japan; it was the beginning of the end. By July, the tonnage dropped on Japan had tripled that of March. LeMay was not only confined to bombing; his aircraft also mined Japanese coastal waters sinking more than one and a quarter million tons of shipping.

The next step was psychological. Civilian morale took a nose-dive after the Tokyo Fire Raids, so LeMay dropped pamphlets advising the populace of the next objective. The air offensive began to tell with over nine million people fleeing into the rural areas. Production on war materials declined sharply. Oil refinery production decreased 83.5 percent; aircraft engine manufacture was down by 75 percent; airframes were down by 60 percent and electronics equipment by over 75 percent – Japan was beaten; all that was left to do was to admit it.

In July 1945 General Carl Spaatz assumed command of the new United States Strategic Air Forces in the Pacific. This consisted of the 5th, 7th, 13th and 20th Air Forces, as well as, 21st Bomber Command. Also with the war in Europe over, units of the 8th Air Force were being redeployed to the Pacific Theater.

The 16 July saw the International Conference open at Potsdam to draw up terms for the surrender of Japan, and to discuss military and political problems connected with ending hostilities. Twentieth Air Force HQ was officially moved to Harmon Field, Guam, and 20th Bomber Command inactivated and 21st Bomber Command absorbed by HQ 20th Air Force; Major General Curtis LeMay assumed command of the reorganized air force. Meanwhile, 466 B-29s flew against Hiratsuka, Kuwana, Numazu and Oita dropping a substantial load of incendiaries. The USAAF was doing everything in its power to bomb Japan into submission.

It was hoped that the Japanese would surrender if a declaration was made defining 'unconditional surrender'. But if no satisfactory response was received, military sanctions would be applied. This meant the entry of Russia into the war, an intensification of air attacks and naval blockade, and finally the use of the atomic bomb. Russia's declaration of war would have little effect upon the Japanese home islands or change the uncompromising positions of Japanese military leaders, unless defeated on home ground. Air attacks could not be intensified until more airfields were built on Okinawa and new air units deployed; the blockade was already complete and for the

Above: *PFC JJ Topf cleans the paws of Butch, the mascot of Ordnance Section, 364th Service Group while Brownie awaits his turn.*
Below: *A B-24 leaves the flaming beachhead of Iwo Jima.*

most part highly successful. This only left one choice, the atomic bomb. Considered objectively its use would compel the Japanese leaders to see that surrender was their only hope if they wished to avoid wholesale slaughter. Furthermore the use of the atomic bomb would permit selective destruction rather than the wholesale devastation of a prolonged war and save numerous American lives.

The 20 July saw the 509th Composite Group begin a series of twelve precision attacks over Japan for familiarization purposes with tactics contemplated for scheduled atomic strikes. While the 509th practiced, 75 B-29s were busy hitting the oil refinery and petroleum center at Kawasaki and another 29 B-29s mined waters at Fushiki, Nanao, Pusan, Obama and Sustin.

On 30 July, Japan's military leaders decided with their usual stubborn attitude to ignore the Potsdam Declaration and to carry on fighting. The Potsdam Conference resulted in the United States being left to carry the ball in the Pacific. It was decided that some means of saving Japanese honor and an assurance for their future should be given in an attempt to end the war without further bloodshed.

On 1 August 627 B-29s fire-bombed the Japanese cities of Hachioji, Mito, Nagaoka and Toyama; 120 others hit the Kawasaki petroleum plants; and 37 more deep mines in the Nakaumi Lagoon, the Shimonoseki Strait, at Sakai, Seishim and Yonago. This was the largest single-day effort by the 20th Air Force for the entire war, a total of 836 B-29s dispatched.

General Nathan Twining became 20th Air Force commander, on 2 August 1945, and LeMay became Chief of Staff, USASTAF. The 20th and Far East Air Force kept continuous pressure on the Japanese hoping against hope that the sort of punishment they were dishing out would end the war. But the Japanese military leaders were not ready to capitulate. The only choice left to the United States Government was to show Japan that they meant business. On 6 August 1945 the first atomic bomb was dropped over Hiroshima, a city of 345,000 and the HQ of the Japanese Second General Army and numerous military

Below: *A North American P-51 named* Alp Girl *takes off from Iwo Jima in the Bonin Islands, a base which also sent and serviced the escorts for B-29s.*

Left: *An atomic bomb destroys Nagasaki on 9 August 1945.*
Right: *The USS* Pennslyvania *(BB-38) fires her forward guns, Leyte, October 1944.*

establishments. At 0815hrs the bomb was dropped accurately by Colonel Paul Tibbets, flying in the *Enola Gay*, a B-29 of the 393rd Bomb Squadron, 509th Composite Group. The results were 78,000 dead, 48,000 wounded, 176,000 people made homeless, and over 70,000 buildings and structures destroyed. This was caused by a single 9000lb atomic device and which ushered in the nuclear age. President Harry Truman in a broadcast on 7 August said that as long as Japan did not comply with surrender terms, similar atomic bombs would be dropped elsewhere in Japan.

The Japanese leaders now saw the need for surrender but were unable to agree on acceptable terms. The Supreme Japanese Council was still arguing when at 1130hrs, on 9 August 1945, the second atomic bomb was exploded on Nagasaki, a city of 270,000. The credit for the second bomb was erroneously given to one of the observation planes, *The Great Artiste*. The device was dropped by Captain F Bock's *Bockscar*, and it was not until after the war that the mix-up was discovered and set right. The result was another 35,000 dead, and 60,000 wounded. It is interesting to note what others overlook; in the Great Tokyo Fire Raid, 9–10 March 1945, 84,000 died and 40,000 were wounded. Still the Supreme Council was divided and the decision was left to the Emperor who agreed on 10 August to the Allied terms.

MacArthur's superb island-hopping strategy conducted in the Pacific Theater by the Allied Forces was undertaken primarily to acquire installations for B-29 operations against Japan. With the establishment of these bases, the B-29s of the 20th Air Force were unleashed, systematically destroying

Below: *The drydock at Kure, Japan held about 59 two-man submarines and was badly bombed.*

3D-198
3D-135

Previous page: *Wrecked Japanese aircraft lie undisturbed at Atsugi Airport, Japan, in September 1945.*

Japan's main industrial and military centers one by one using incendiaries. The Japanese buildings were tightly packed and lightly constructed which made them extremely vulnerable to this type of attack. The destruction in built-up areas alone amounted to 99.7 percent.

Besides these totally devastating attacks against strategic targets, the B-29s were simultaneously employed on a highly successful campaign of mine-laying in Japanese home waters, which applied an economic and tactical noose around the home islands of Japan. The two atomic bombs dropped on Hiroshima and Nagasaki were the *coup de grâce* to insure a swift conclusion to the war but the B-29 was a major factor responsible for the defeat and unconditional surrender of Japan.

For the first time in recorded history, a major power was defeated primarily by the use of air power. Japan's unconditional surrender bears mute witness to this fact. This was the supreme and ultimate moment for the proponents of strategic bombing. Some notable critics of the strategic bombing believed the atomic bomb solely responsible for the surrender of Japan. But even before the use of the atomic bombs, strategic bombing had so depleted Japanese war production that key industries were totally disrupted. The end result was unbelievable: 733,000 casualties of whom 300,000 were dead, and over 9,220,000 people were without homes. This destruction was caused by the US strategic bombing force and is considered the primary factor in causing the Japanese people to feel unwilling to continue fighting a hopeless cause.

B-29 Superfortress

Length: 99ft
Height: 27ft 9in
Wing area: 1736sq ft
Span: 141ft 3in
Max speed: 357mph at 30,000ft
Max speed: 306mph at sea level
Max load: 60,500lbs
Max overload: 135,000lbs
Economical cruise speed: 220mph at 25,000ft
Initial climb rate: 900ft/min
Ceiling: 33,600ft
Weight empty: 74,500lbs
Armament: 12 ×0.5in machine guns, in four remote-controlled turrets and in the tail, each with 1000rds of ammo and one 20mm cannon firing rearward.
Engines: Four Wright-Cyclone, R-3350-23, 18 cylinder air-cooled radial engines, each with two General Electric turbo-superchargers rated at 2200hp for take off and 2300hp under emergency conditions.

Above left: *A B-29 is refueled before resuming its tasks.*
Above: *The main business district of Kobe, Japan was damaged by bombs.*
Below: *Atomic devastation as seen from 'zero' target, of Hiroshima, Japan.*

Conclusion

The United States' Army Air Force's contribution to the successful conclusion of the war was tremendous. It is extremely difficult to show only one service's contribution without involving the others. A combination of air, land and sea power was required and World War II saw the foundations firmly laid for Combined Operations.

As far as the Strategic Bombing Offensive is concerned, it was the most direct single factor which forced Hitler onto the defensive by robbing his armies of irreplaceable air support. The effect of this change from offensive to defensive obviously benefited the Russians but they also benefited the other fronts as well, forming the ring which eventually choked Germany.

The offensive was a jockeying for position and authority between RAF Bomber Command under Harris and the US 8th Air Force under Eaker. Harris firmly believed the bombing of Germany would be an American controlled offensive. As it turned out, Bomber Command remained an independent air force with a totally different strategy from its US counterparts. This was due to the failure of the 8th Air Force in 1943 to achieve its goals comprehensively. The air operations of 1942 against targets in France and the Low Countries gave absolutely no hint of what was going to happen over Germany, culminating in that one week in October 1943, when one-third of 8th Bomber Command was destroyed.

Regardless of heavy armament the B-17 was not a viable proposition without a long-range fighter to escort it. Billy Mitchell and all the major proponents of strategic bombing never envisioned that the bomber would succeed alone and unprotected. These men held that to be successful in a deep penetration raid, the bombers should be given adequate fighter protection to prevent crippling losses. The Schweinfurt Raids proved this point irrevocably. A long-range fighter had to be developed or they would not have been able to continue attacks at all. So the P-51 Mustang entered the scene and out went the self-defending bomber. The Schweinfurt raids were so significant that the entire Allied Combined Bombing Offensive was placed on the chopping block.

The United States theory of unescorted daylight precision bombing was shot to hell by the Luftwaffe's fighter command, which gave the RAF Bomber Command a new lease on life. The fortunes of the two air forces are usually obscured by accounts of what is called the Combined Bomber Offensive; an operation intended to achieve Anglo-American 'command of the air' through the destruction of the Luftwaffe. Except for the short period leading up to D-Day on 6 June 1944, there was no combined bomber offensive. In reality there were two separate and distinct offensives: the Royal Air Force carried out area bombing by night, the Americans precision daylight bombing. There was no coordination of effort as shown by the Schweinfurt Raids because the British refused to bomb it. But despite the heavy losses of 1943, US airmen believed in the principles of concentrated attacks on industrialized targets.

By January 1944 a real Combined Bombing Offensive evolved, mainly due to a 'rethink' after the Schweinfurt raids. In February came the combined attack on Schweinfurt but without American pressure for continued daylight precision bombing, air superiority would not have been attained over the skies of Europe, and the Normandy invasion would not have been possible. The main discovery was air strategists no longer talked about how the strategic bomber would win the war singlehanded.

The most vital effect of the US bombing campaign was that it drew off a tremendous proportion of Germany's fighter forces from the Eastern Front, thus indirectly aiding the Russian advance. In August 1943, Field Marshal Erhard Milch stated that a large force of Jagdgruppen were being recalled from other areas to defend the Reich from enemy air raids. The total Luftwaffe strength in the west rose from 1687 to 2097 aircraft but overall it fell from 5396 to 4830. Once the Germans were required to withdraw their forces from other fronts to defend the Fatherland they were inevitably doomed.

The strategic bomber did not defeat Hitler's Reich on its own, as its proponents believed, but it had played a most decisive part. The single most important contribution of the strategic bomber to the defeat of Germany was the elimination of 97 percent of her petroleum supplies. To accomplish this 130,000 tons of bombs had been dropped by US bombers on oil targets. The bomber also tied down over one million German troops manning the air defenses of the Reich. Overall the cost was extremely high: 6378 crews and 8314 bombers. The number of Germans who died as a result of bombing missions was over 350,000 and 800,000 were wounded.

The strategic bomber had accomplished one very definite result, a radical step forward in the modernization of warfare. It saw the true beginning of total war and the new more powerful weaponry allowed no discrimination between combatant and non-combatant. Fear has always been a part of war, but never before had it been instilled in the hearts of the people to the degree brought about by the strategic bombings as shown by surveys taken at the end of the war.

Air power was a decisive factor in winning the war in Europe and Japan. It could have been employed differently but it was truly decisive, its victory complete. Combined with naval power it ended the U-Boat threat; on land, it turned the tide in favor of Allied ground forces. It was directly responsible for the success of the Normandy invasion and subsequent breakout at St Lô. It helped destroy the economic backbone of the Reich which brought about its eventual collapse. It represented modern warfare with all its horror and suffering, the vivid impact of which the German and Japanese people will never forget.

A first-class military power cannot survive with a full-scale strategic air offensive over its industrial heart. By early 1945, Germany was at the end of its tether. Armament production had fallen irretrievably and total disintegration followed. Germany had sustained a mortal wound. The offensive forced Germany to utilize their scarce resources on air defense, to build

fighters which delayed their top secret rocket program. In the end they had to use horses for transport.

Directly after World War II, a great debate ensued, on exactly how effective strategic bombing really was in ending the war. One school of thought stated that the Combined Bombing Offensive against Germany produced limited long-range results, too few for the cost entailed. Whether or not it was successful against Germany is a debatable issue but it was unquestionably successful against Japan. The Japanese knew they were defeated even before the first atomic bombs were dropped.

The US Chiefs of Staff expected the invasion of Japan to be contested bitterly, and to be extremely costly in American casualties. Although the Japanese Air Force and Navy were practically totally destroyed and large numbers of their prime troops isolated in the Western Pacific, there were still sufficient quantities of combat troops left, with the unshakeable conviction that to surrender was unthinkable, to insure great carnage and unnecessary deaths to the US forces landing on Japanese home islands.

The strategic bombing offensive against Japan, which reached a savage crescendo in November 1944, made it easier for the Emperor to intervene personally at the end. The question remains, 'Were the two atomic weapons dropped on Hiroshima and Nagasaki really necessary?' To answer that question you must also ask yourself whether an atomic bomb is worse than the fire raids which were already devastating Japan on a daily basis.

The worst attack on a city during the war, and the worst of all time, was the Tokyo Fire Raid of 9–10 March 1945. A force of 520 B-29s dropped 4000 tons of incendiary clusters on a sector encompassing eleven square miles. This raid resulted in a civilian casualty rate between 80,000 and 100,000. The majority of these died from asphyxiation. Hiroshima was also tragic, although administered with clinical efficiency, but it was not more devastating than the Tokyo Fire Raid. The bombing was the single most important factor in making the Japanese people feel unwilling to continue the war.

The men who were directly responsible for the recommendation of the atomic bomb were: Secretary of War, Henry L Stimson, and four of the developers Drs Arthur H Compton, Enrico Fermi, E O Lawrence and J R Oppenheimer. All things taken into consideration, I can find no fault with their recommendation or the decision which ultimately rested squarely on the shoulders of President Harry S Truman.

World War II saw the USAAF come of age. What it previously lacked in experienced staff planners and organizers, it now both had in abundance. The men who saw it through controversy, setback and final victory were now ready, willing and more than able to take the next step – independence as a separate branch of the armed forces. These leaders saw the development of weapons like the P-47 Thunderbolt, P-51 Mustang, B-17 Flying Fortress, B-24 Liberator and B-29 Super Fortress and many others during the war years, things which airmen had previously only dreamed about.

It was airmen and pioneers like Foulois, Mitchell, Arnold, Andrews, Spaatz, Twining, Eaker, Hansell, Doolittle and LeMay who believed that the strength of our great nation lay in the air and these far-sighted men were right. The USAAF proved itself during World War II, which culminated in the National Defense Act of 18 September 1947, making the United States Air Force, independent and an integral part of the Defense structure. This was a just reward and one long overdue.

The United States Army Air Force
had numerous compliments paid to it but the greatest
was by Winston Spencer Churchill:

'They never flinched or failed.
It is to their devotion that in no small measure
we owe our victory'.

INSIGNIA

First Air Force

American Theater

Second Air Force

American Theater

Third Air Force

Anti-submarine, American Theater

Fourth Air Force

American Theater

Fifth Air Force

Philippine Islands
East Indies
Air Offensive, Japan
China Defensive
Papua
New Guinea
Northern Solomons
Bismark Archipelago
Western Pacific
Leyte
Luzon
Southern Philippines
China Offensive

Sixth Air Force

Anti-submarine, American Theater

Seventh Air Force

Central Pacific
Air Offensive, Japan
Eastern Mandates
Western Pacific
Ryukyus
China Offensive

Eighth Air Force

(originally VII Bomber Command)

Air Offensive, Europe
Normandy
Northern France
Rhineland
Ardennes–Alsace
Central Europe
Asiatic–Pacific Theater

Ninth Air Force

American Theater
Air Combat, EAME Theater
Egypt–Libya
Air Offensive, Europe
Tunisia
Sicily
Naples–Foggia
Normandy
Northern France
Rhineland
Ardennes–Alsace
Central Europe

Tenth Air Force

Burma, 1942
India–Burma
China Defensive
Central Burma
China Offensive

Eleventh Air Force

Air Offensive, Japan
Aleutian Islands

Twelfth Air Force

Air Combat, EAME Theater
Algeria–French Morocco
Tunisia
Sicily
Naples–Foggia
Anzio
Rome–Arno
Southern France
North Apennines
Po Valley

Thirteenth Air Force

China, Defensive,
Guadalcanal
New Guinea
Northern Solomons
Eastern Mandates
Bismarck Archipelago
Western Pacific
Leyte
Luzon
Southern Philippines
China Offensive

Fourteenth Air Force

India–Burma
China Defensive
China Offensive

Fifteenth Air Force

Air Combat, EAME Theater
Air Offensive, Europe
Naples–Foggia
Anzio
Rome-Arno
Normandy
Northern France
Southern France
North Apennines
Rhineland
Central Europe
Po Valley

Twentieth Air Force

American Theater
India–Burma
Air Offensive, Japan
China Defensive
Eastern Mandates
Western Pacific
Central Burma

US Strategic Air Forces in Europe

(originally Eighth Air Force)

Air Combat, EAME Theater
Air Offensive Europe
Normandy
Northern France
Rhineland
Ardennes–Alsace
Central Europe

INDEX

AIRCRAFT

SELECTED BIBLIOGRAPHY

The Air Plan That Defeated Hitler, Brigadier General Haywood S Hansell

History of the United States Air Force 1907–1957, US Strategic Bombing Survey (various reports)

Army Air Forces in World War II, Craven and Cate

Air Force Combat Units of World War II, Maurer and Maurer

Air Force Combat Squadrons of World War II, Maurer and Maurer

The Story of the USSBS, David MacIsaac

The Army Air Forces in World War II (A Combat Chronology 1941–1945), Carson and Mueller

Air Force Magazine

The Airpower Historian

The RAF Yearbook

ACKNOWLEDGMENTS

The author would like to thank the following individuals who assisted or provided information and material for the preparation of this book:

Syd Mayer, my good friend and mentor

Joseph Whitt, PhD, whose sound advice was invaluable

Vern Burke, 3rd Air Force historian

Charlie Gallagher, Founder of the Friends of the Eighth

Charles G Worman, Air Force Museum

Albert F Simpson, Historical Research Center of the Imperial War Museum, London

Richard Natkiel who prepared the maps

Michael Badrocke who contributed the technical drawings

David Eldred who designed the book

The author is also grateful to the United States Air Force which provided all the photographs for this book except for the following:

USIS: 21 (center)

US Navy: 86–87, 89.

National Archives: 97, 98, 174 (top)

Bison Picture Library: 99 (both)

Robert Hunt Library: 167 (top)